10/10/98

Dad,

Happy birthday 1998.
Maybe you'll come and see the Australian baobabs one day!

Timothy
x x

THE BOAB TREE PAT LOWE

Lothian
BOOKS

pen and ink illustrations: Huw Crompton
front cover photograph: Boab at El Questro Station,
East Kimberley, Western Australia
back cover: Ancient Boab on the flood plain
near Wyndham, Western Australia
COVER PHOTOS: Bill Bachman
TEXT PHOTOS: Bill Bachman, Gill Burt, Pat Lowe
endpapers: The Forrest Tree

Thomas C. Lothian Pty Ltd
11 Munro Street, Port Melbourne, Victoria 3207

Copyright © Pat Lowe 1998
First published 1998

All rights reserved. No part of this publication
may be reproduced, stored in a retrieval system
or transmitted in any form by any means without
the prior permission of the copyright owner.
Enquiries should be made to the publisher.

National Library of Australia
Cataloguing-in-Publication data:

Lowe, Pat, 1941–.
 The boab tree.
 ISBN 0 85091 912 6.
 1. Baobab – Western Australian. 2. Baobab –
Northern Territory. I. Title.
583.68

Design by Tony Gilevski
Printed in Hong Kong by South China Printing

The Keep River National Park,
Northern Territory

contents

Acknowledgements PAGE 4

Introduction PAGE 5

CHAPTER 1   Mysterious Beginnings PAGE 9

CHAPTER 2   Sex, Reproduction and Death PAGE 23

CHAPTER 3   A Tree of the People PAGE 37

CHAPTER 4   The Familiar PAGE 53

CHAPTER 5   The Famous PAGE 63

CHAPTER 6   Home Life PAGE 79

MAP   The Eight Baobabs of the World PAGE 93

Bibliography PAGE 94

Index PAGE 95

acknowledgements

This book could not have been written without the help and encouragement of many people. Special thanks go to:

Wendy Albert of the Kimberley Bookshop for helping get me started, for her insistence I 'hurry up and finish it!' and for finding me a publisher. I know she will also be the most enthusiastic retailer of this book.

Tim Willing and Kim Akerman for their unstinting generosity with information and ideas, for pointing me in the direction of published material, and for providing me with papers and photographs. They both read the completed manuscript, discussed some of the scientific questions and made valuable suggestions. Tim allowed me full access to his own collection of Boab material, and often turned up at my door with a new reference. Kim kept my fax running hot.

Alex George for his careful reading of an early draft of the manuscript, for his suggestions and for sparing me the embarrassment of a number of errors.

Jane Lodge for her generous early efforts at turning the manuscript into a draft book. Jane also came to the rescue at the last minute to compose the page of maps.

Jimmy Pike who accompanied me on a number of my Boab journeys, prevented me from getting lost, and on more than one occasion was kept awake as I shone torches into Boab trees and enthused about the opening flowers.

Space does not allow me to detail here the contribution of every person who helped me, but the text often reveals what that was. I am grateful to Glenice Allan, Patrick Armstrong, Gordon Barunga, Peter Bibby, Stumpy Brown, the late Manuela Burrwan, Gill Burt, Max Clarke, Huw Crompton, Chris Done, Russell Hanigan, Perpetua Hobcroft, Harry Hooper, Dennis Howard, Margaret Howard, the Kimberley Land Council, Gwen Knox, Daisy Lungunan, Dr Bernadette Masters, Alison Morris, Ian and Terri Obern, Mary Pandilo, Biddy Simon, Alison Spencer, John Watson, G. E. Wickens, John Woodman and Matthew Wrigley.

introduction

Some years ago I came across a slim book called *Tree of Life*. It is a children's picture book about the African Baobab tree, written and illustrated by Barbara Bash.

I could immediately see in my mind's eye the Australian version of such a book. I imagined Kimberley school children setting off, book in hand, on natural history excursions to examine Boab trees and explore their history and their ecology. I told anyone who would listen, 'Someone should write a book about the Boab tree!' I even wrote to Barbara Bash to suggest she write a companion to her *Tree of Life*, but she didn't leap to oblige. No one did.

Eventually, perhaps tired of listening to me, my friend Wendy Albert said, 'Why don't you write it?' Still stuck on my vision of an Australian version of Bash's book, I said, 'I couldn't: I can't draw!' But the idea germinated. I could not produce a book like Bash's, but I could write one of my own. Someone else could do the illustrations. That I knew next to nothing about Boab trees did not daunt me: the best way to learn about something is to write a book about it.

As soon as I had decided to take up the challenge, I became excited. It gave me an excuse to spend a lot of time thinking about and looking at Boab trees. I went to libraries and read about them. I ordered scientific papers. I studied history books. I spoke to native Kimberley people, and to botanists. I made new friends and badgered old ones. I undertook a course in botany at the local TAFE. At weekends I would drive off in my Suzuki and spent whole days around, in and under Boab trees. Certain ones became as familiar as old friends. I gave some of them names. I camped amongst them to watch them flower and to see what lived in them. I probed their cavities. Boab trees became an obsession, almost a secret vice. They will undoubtedly remain so.

introduction

I recorded all these activities in notebooks, which were the source of much of the material in this book. Writing it has been one of the great pleasures of my life.

I have tried to ensure that the information contained in this book is accurate, and where possible I have written from my own experience and research. Second-hand stories I have questioned and checked where I could. I have done my best to solve mysteries created by inconsistent reports in other texts. While I have had to take the botanical information on trust, it is drawn from the most recent work of experts in the field. The bias towards trees of the West Kimberley occurs because that is where I live. All the ecological observations, and any errors, are my own.

In late 1996 I met Huw Crompton in Broome, an artist who specialises in Baobab trees around the world. He has seen, drawn and painted every species. We talked about collaboration, and then Huw left for overseas. He returned to Broome in the nick of time, on New Year's Eve 1997, shortly before my publication deadline, and worked hard to complete his drawings. They enhance the book in a way far beyond my expectations.

opposite: Ord River, East Kimberley, Western Australia

mysterious beginnings | Chapter 1

The Australian Boab tree stands out, a colossus amongst the trees of the north-western Australian bush. Though not exceptionally tall as trees go, it has few competitors for height within its own habitat. And it is not the height so much as the girth and the gothic form of these trees as they advance in age that so impresses the observer. Even the smaller, younger Boabs are remarkable for their bottle shapes; their wide, smooth, grey or sometimes bronze trunks taper upwards to a narrow neck from which the boughs branch up and outwards. Some individual Boab trees are amongst the oldest living things on this continent today, and amongst the oldest living things on earth. It is probable that the same trees were already standing where they are now before the time of Mohammed, before the time of Christ. For centuries they have been landmarks, their burly presence dwarfing the surrounding bush.

Yet, despite their antiquity, the Boabs seem like strangers in the land-

above: Panton River, East Kimberley, WA
opposite: An aged Boab near the Broome–Derby road, its fibrous trunk now completely hollow, still producing new growth

mysterious beginnings | Chapter 1

scape. The Kimberley bush of Western Australia consists, for the most part, of small, drought-resistant, rough-barked evergreen trees, wattle scrub, and grasslands. Though this first-glance uniformity is deceptive, and conceals a wealth of subtly varied habitats, the profile of the vegetation is low. The massive Boabs, their trunks swathed in folds of grey bark, are more like vegetable elephants than regular members of the region's flora.

The Australian Boab's closest relations do not live in Australia, but far away across the Indian Ocean. Madagascar, that long, large island off the east coast of Africa, is the true home of the Baobab, from which name the word Boab derives. There are six species of Baobab in Madagascar, and only two others in the rest of the world. One of these is the African Baobab, *Adansonia digitata*, the other the Australian Boab tree, *A. gregorii*.

How, then, did the Boab tree come to be living in Australia? It is a different species from all the other seven, and so it cannot simply have been introduced from Madagascar or from Africa. It has been here long enough to have evolved into its present distinct form.

arrival

Nobody knows for sure how the Boab's ancestors arrived in the north of Australia, but there are two major hypotheses. One of these suggests that a species of Baobab was already established on the part of Gondwanaland that was to become the north-western tip of Australia before continental drift broke up that huge supercontinent into separate lands somewhere between 160 and 50 million years ago.* However, most scientists now believe that Baobabs are not an ancient enough genus for this to have been the case. Despite their antediluvian appearance, Baobabs have floral characteristics of relatively recent evolution. Furthermore, a distribution dating from Gondwanaland would be expected to include the lands intervening between Africa and Australia such as the Arabian peninsula and the Indian sub-

*Authorities vary wildly in their estimates of that period.

continent, which fall within the latitudes favoured by Baobabs. Yet Baobabs do not occur naturally in these places.

Another serious objection to the Gondwanaland hypothesis is the extreme variations that have occurred in Australia's latitude and therefore climate since separation from Gondwanaland: changes that have not been paralleled in Madagascar. No Baobab species could have tolerated and survived relatively unchanged what botanist Patrick Armstrong calls the 'climatic gyrations' to which this continent has been subjected.

An alternative plausible explanation for the appearance of Boab trees on the Australian continent, which scientists such as Armstrong now think more likely, is perhaps also the most interesting: that the Australian Boab's ancestor was a species of Baobab from Madagascar whose seeds arrived in a nut that floated here across the Indian Ocean.

Ocean transport of species is not uncommon. *Gyrocarpus americanus*, the Corkwood or Helicopter Tree with its winged fruits so beloved of children, is a frequent companion of the Boab in northern Australia. Different subspecies of the same tree are associated with other Baobabs in Madagascar and Africa. They are also present in India and Central America. Such a wide distribution over four continents is almost certainly due to long distance dispersal by sea.

There are several reasons for accepting the flotation hypothesis for the Boab tree. Madagascar, an island on which so many species of Baobab are concentrated, does appear to be the cradle of the Baobab genus, and is surely the major locus of its evolution into separate forms.

Baobab trees in Madagascar, as elsewhere, are often associated with water. The nuts do float, and are often dispersed in streams and rivers within the island. It is probable that some of these nuts are carried out to sea, and a

THE EIGHT BAOBABS OF THE WORLD

Adansonia fony
Fony
Madagascar

Adansonia perrieri
Bozy
northern Madagascar

Adansonia digitata
African Baobab
sub-Saharan Africa

Adansonia suarezensis
Bozybe
northern Madagascar

Adansonia madagascariensis
Bozy
northern madagascar

Adansonia gregorii
Australian Boab
Kimberley, Australia

Adansonia grandidieri (west)
Renala
western Madagascar

Adansonia grandidieri (south)
Renala
western Madagascar

Adansonia za
Za
south-west Madagascar

mysterious beginnings | Chapter 1

few of them may have drifted with the currents across the Indian Ocean, to fetch up on the nearest landfall, the north-west coast of Australia. At the time such an event is thought to have happened, Africa and its island, Madagascar, were still much closer to Australia than they are now, so the nuts would not have had as far to travel as they would if they were to make a similar journey today. That the immediate ancestor of our Boab was Malagasy rather than African is indicated by the greater similarities of *A. gregorii* with *A. madagascariensis* and other insect-pollinated island species than with the bat-pollinated *A. digitata*.

Yet another possibility, proposed by Lusaka botanist Mike Bingham, that *Adansonia* first evolved in Africa, differentiated into separate species on the island of Madagascar, and sent a single scion across the Indian Ocean to Australia, is not supported by the genetic evidence. The most recent genetic work on the genus shows *A. digitata* to have a far higher chromosome count than any of the other species, higher counts being associated with more recent development. Far from being the oldest and most primitive, *A. digitata* may be the most recently evolved of the eight species.

Even if found to be correct, Bingham's hypothesis does not diminish the mystery of *Adansonia*'s arrival in Australia. Long distance dispersal across the Indian Ocean, either directly from Madagascar or via a staging post on the now submerged islands of the Ninety East Ridge in the eastern Indian Ocean, remains the most probable means.

The present distribution of the Boab is consistent with this scenario. The tree has so far become established naturally only in the extreme north-west of the Australian continent, and it appears to have spread from the coastal west, inland towards the east.

Although such a means of dispersal may sound unlikely, particularly in view of prevailing currents and winds which have been found to carry

Indonesian seeds west rather than east, Baobab seeds would not be the only ones known to have drifted east across the Indian Ocean.

The Coco de Mer palm of the Seychelles Islands is one plant whose seeds, carried in huge buoyant pods, have been found washed up on the shores of Western Australia.

An even more unlikely arrival from Madagascar discovered on the coast of Western Australia is an enormous and ancient egg from the now extinct Elephant Bird (*Aepyornis* sp.). This fossilised egg, found in 1993 in a sand dune near Cervantes, and a similar one, found at Scott River near Augusta in 1930, are thought to be several thousand years old. Furthermore, two relatively fresh King Penguin eggs, probably laid two thousand kilometres away by birds living on the Kerguelen Islands in the southern Indian Ocean, have also been found on the shores of Western Australia.

While other seeds and eggs floating across the Indian Ocean to Australia do not prove that the same thing happened to the Baobab, they certainly demonstrate that such a journey is possible. And we know that it is normal for Baobab pods to be dispersed by water, which is more than can be said about eggs.

Whatever its means of arrival, the seed germinated, and once the tree started to grow it found the conditions in Australia unlike, but not too unlike, those in its home territory. The Devonian reef limestone country of the Kimberley has similarities with the pinnacled *tsingy* plateaux of western and north-western Madagascar, and the two regions have in common red-earth landscapes.

When the tree came into flower it was pollinated by different, but not too different, species of insects and birds from those that had pollinated its ancestors. But pollinated it was; the first obstacles to survival had been overcome.

mysterious beginnings | Chapter 1

When it dropped its fruit, the seeds germinated, but they needed to do more than simply grow in the shadow of their parent. To colonise their new country, they had to be dispersed. And dispersed they were. Local conditions had many subtle effects on the the tree's development, some of which we will examine later. Gradually, over hundreds and then thousands of years, its descendants were reshaped, and the Boab tree of northern Australia became the unique species that we know today.

name

The name Baobab is of Arab origin. Prospero Alpino, a Venetian herbalist, found the imported fruit of *A. digitata* on sale in the Cairo herb and spice markets, and in 1592 he recorded its name there as *bu hobab*. Botanist G. E. Wickens, in his scholarly little book about 'Africa's Upside-Down Tree', points out that the similar sounding *bu hibab* means 'the fruit with many seeds' and considers this the most likely origin of the European term 'Baobab'.

The genus of Baobabs was first given its botanical name *Adansonia* after the French naturalist, Michel Adanson. Adanson's teacher, Bernard de Jussieu, proposed the name and it was adopted by the great Swedish taxonomist, Linnaeus, who, in his descriptive work, *Species Plantarum*, first described *A. digitata* for science in 1753. At that time the African species was the only known member of the genus. Adanson preferred to use the name Baobab, but the rules of scientific nomenclature require the first published name to be adopted. Both terms remain in use, one common, the other scientific.

The naming of the Australian species was less straightforward. Allan Cunningham, naturalist on the HMC *Mermaid* in the 1820s, saw specimens in the course of the *Mermaid's* voyage to northern Australia, and mistakenly assigned them to the Capparis genus, naming the tree *Capparis gibbosa*. It was given its now familiar name, *Adansonia gregorii*, by Ferdinand Mueller

mysterious beginnings | Chapter 1

(later Baron von Mueller), the botanist who first recognised it as belonging to the same genus as the African Baobab. Mueller named the species in honour of Augustus Charles Gregory, commander of the North Australian Exploring Expedition of 1855–56, of which Mueller was a member. However, because of the earlier publication of the specific name *gibbosa* in Cunningham's natural history appendix to the report by *Mermaid*'s Captain Phillip Parker King, Harvard botanist David Baum argues that the Australian Boab should now be known as *Adansonia gibbosa*

Kununurra, WA

mysterious beginnings | Chapter 1

PAGE 18 Young Boab, Ivanhoe, East Kimberley, WA

mysterious beginnings | Chapter 1

in accordance with the rules of priority in taxonomy. This proposed reversion to the earlier specific name is not yet accepted by Australian taxonomists, who are making a case to retain the name by which the species has always been known.

While there is much to be said for retaining a name that everyone is used to, Augustus Gregory had nothing whatever to do with the tree's discovery or identification, and Mueller had a lamentable habit of naming species for his patrons and friends. The term *gibbosa*, meaning swollen, has the virtue of describing the tree, but as the quality of swollenness is shared by all members of the genus, this name is no more distinctive than its alternative.

Until very recently, the origin of the Baobab from which the Boab descends was a matter of conjecture. The most likely closest relation was *A. madagascariensis*, because of similarities in flower structure and major pollinators. More recently, *A. madagascariensis* has been shown also to have the closest genetic relationship with the Australian tree. This relationship has been demonstrated practically by Broome botanist Tim Willing, who grafted branches from *A. madagascariensis* onto a rootstock of *A. gregorii*. Just three weeks after the graft was made, the first green shoots of leaves appeared at the ends of the grafted branches.

How long do Boab trees live? How old are the biggest ones we see, with the thickest, most gnarled trunks? This is not an easy question to answer because little research has yet been done on the Australian tree, and records do not go back far enough to tell us anything about the early history of the older specimens. In some species of tree, the growth rings through the trunk are a reliable guide to age, but this is not so in the case of the Boab. The

mysterious beginnings | Chapter 1

wood is fibrous, and the rings are not always well defined. Neither are they reliably annual, but may be formed only during seasons of good rainfall when significant growth occurs. Furthermore, the fibrous tissue rots quickly, so that sections cannot be cut and preserved as they can with other species of tree, such as the pines. However, in the absence of direct evidence, we can extrapolate from what is known about the Boab's African relation.

Carbon dating of a moderately large specimen of the African Baobab, *A. digitata*, felled in 1960, gave an age estimate of around one thousand years. Comparison between its inner and outer wood suggested that the tree grows more slowly as it ages, and the investigator, E. R. Swart, concluded that 'there appears to be no reason why some of the really large baobabs should not be several thousand years old'. David Livingstone counted the growth rings of some large specimens, the oldest of which he estimated to be over four thousand years of age, but this figure has never been confirmed. Certainly, trees of this genus are capable of living for many centuries.

Logue River trees
Some slim young trees in a well-known stand of Boabs near Logue River on the Broome–Derby road clearly have a long way to go before they reach even average size. Yet men who worked as stockmen in the district thirty years ago remember them then looking much as they do today. Certain older trees nearby, wide and gnarled and bent, used to provide shade over dinner camps for the same young men who nowadays make their journeys by car, and sometimes use them still.

One massive tree, surely an ancestor of all the other trees in the Logue River grove, sprawls on the bank of a billabong a few hundred metres from the road. This old Grandmother still flowers and bears fruit, as it must have been doing every year for centuries past. With a trunk as broad as it is high, this specimen seems to me less like a tree than like a woody village.

mysterious beginnings | Chapter 1

A visitor could spend hours exploring the many cavities that pit its trunk and examining the invertebrate life that has made use of them.

Spiders spin webbing nests in some hollows; bagmoths, pupating in their costumes of grass or mud, cluster in others. Here mason wasps find all they need: mud and water for building their nests, and crannies in which to conceal them.

Underneath the thick and serpentine roots, in the wet season, you might find a deep burrow dug by one of the huge goannas, known locally as Barni, that live there and prey on the other animal life that is drawn to the billabong.

One day I found a dozen tiny insectivorous bats in a cavity left by a fallen branch, packed together so tightly it was hard to distinguish one from another. Dopey with sleep, they barely reacted to my forefinger gently stroking their velvety heads.

Thick and serpentine roots

sex, reproduction and death | Chapter 2

There are two distinct images that most Kimberley and Territory people have of Boab trees: laden with rich green foliage in the wet season; and bare, with twisted, fingered branches exposed in the dry. Like its frequent companion the Corkwood or Helicopter Tree, *Gyrocarpus americanus*, the Boab is deciduous. It starts to shed its leaves in the early dry season, at the time its fruit are developing, so that when the nuts are ripe and ready to be picked or to fall, the branches are usually bare. The tree stays that way for several months, as a protection against drought, and that is how most tourists see and remember it.

foliage

The first green shoots appear during the hot weather before the rains, in late October. This early leafing, shared by all members of the genus, is not unique to Baobab trees, but for them it serves a special purpose. These trees die if their roots become waterlogged, and this can happen if they experience wet conditions when they have no leaves to carry away the water by transpiration. Putting out their leaves before the wet season ensures that the first heavy rains will not kill them.

Over the next few weeks the tree becomes transformed. The dry, grey, apparently lifeless limbs are rejuvenated by a sudden burst of new foliage. The mature, hand-sized, compound leaves, with from five to seven leaflets, are a brilliant emerald green.

Into this wealth of young leaves come the flowers. Elongated buds appear at the very ends of branches, tough-sepalled and as yet without nectar to discourage thieves. Boab blossoms are a pale, creamy yellow, and the petals have a waxy sheen. Examine a petal under a magnifying glass and you will see that its outer surface is covered with a fine fur. Within the corolla sits a brush of stamens, in the centre of which stands a prominent, star-shaped stigma, borne on a thick style. Some of the flowers grow upright in the tree,

flowers

opposite: Fallen giant

sex, reproduction and death | Chapter 2

but many tilt sideways, or lie more or less horizontal. A few even hang downwards. They seem determined to try out every angle from which they might be pollinated.

If you examine the fully opened flowers closely, you will notice that the petals have rolled back, allowing the central staminal brush the greatest possible freedom in its quest for pollinators. 'Take *me*, take *me!*' it seems to say. If you look at them in the daytime, the flowers may appear a little worn or spent. Some may be turning brown or hanging loose from the tree, ready to fall. This is because the flowers, which only last a single day, bloom at night.

It is worth taking the trouble to watch a Boab's flowers open. The most exciting way of doing this is to camp out overnight close to a tree during the flowering season. Or, if you can find a Boab near where you stay, take a rug to sit on and a strong torch and be prepared to

top: Boab flower fully open
bottom: Screen print of Boab flower by Glenice Allan

sex, reproduction and death | Chapter 2

spend an hour or two beside the tree. Choose one with a number of buds ready to open. These are easy to identify earlier in the day: the long, slim green tube of fused sepals swells and begins to split along the lines scored in its tip, and the spirally compressed petals of palest yellow start to bulge out. The length of emerging flower visible by nightfall may be from two to about eight centimetres.

The hour of opening seems to vary somewhat from place to place, and from tree to tree, as does the speed at which the petals unfold. It may be that the timing is influenced by the phase of the moon. Some time between about seven and nine o'clock at night, the process begins. You will notice that the five sepals, their sharp points already curling backwards, split further down their length, and the tumescent wad of petals continues to thrust forth, and thickens. As the tube opens and they are released from restraint, the petals slowly unfold. Gradually, under pressure from the unfurling flower, the tube splits all the way down to its base. As this happens, the sepals curl right back on themselves allowing the flower freedom to open fully.

Forming a cup shape at first, the petals continue slowly to spread apart. If you watch an opening flower carefully at eye level, you may just perceive the movement of the petals, accompanied by slight jerks as the stamens are liberated and spring into position. The petals, too, fold back on themselves leaving the fluffy brush, the reproductive centre of the flower, fully exposed. Within the calyx a few drops of nectar collect.

Flowers that open at night do so, of course, because night has proved the best time for them to be pollinated. Of the night-flying creatures that might contribute to the pollination of the Boab, David Baum considers hawk-moths possibly the most important. They draw nectar by hovering in front of the flower like tiny hummingbirds, simultaneously inserting their long

pollination

proboscides. As they do so, they bring their heads against the anthers and stigma, collecting and transferring pollen as they feed.

In the early mornings, before sunrise, various species of honey-eaters also come to feed on nectar, and they, too, are probably important pollinators especially when hawkmoths are not present. Often the birds cheat the flowers by stealing the nectar from underneath, forcing their beaks between the calyx and the outside of the petals without touching stamens or picking up pollen at all. However, some birds do keep the age-old bargain between bird and blossom: they push their beaks down inside the corolla, and their heads brush against the pollen-bearing anthers and the stigma.

The African Baobab is known to be pollinated by bats, but it is less certain whether the bats of northern Australia perform the same service for their Boab. I have disturbed bats from a flowering Boab at night, but in the dark it was impossible to tell whether they were after the nectar or the insects feeding on it, and as soon as I shone my torch up into the branches, they flew away. David Baum, who has studied the floral biology of all the world's species of Baobab, thinks bats are unlikely to be major pollinators of the Boab, and he contrasts the pendulous attitude of the African flowers with the more upright bearing of the Australian ones. The floral scent of the Australian tree is sweet, and of a type appreciated by both insects and human beings, whereas bats have a different idea of what smells attractive, a taste to which the African tree unfortunately panders. Furthermore, the Australian flowers hold a much smaller quantity of nectar than do the bat-pollinated African ones, or the Malagasy species pollinated by lemurs. The Australian trees do seem to be catering for insects rather than for mammals.

We should not be surprised that hawkmoths are a major pollinator of Boab trees, for a different species of hawkmoth is known to pollinate the

Boab's closest relation, *A. madagascariensis*. It is dangerous to speculate about events as remote as the germination of the first Baobab seed in Australia, for new knowledge and hindsight can make such speculation seem naive. Nevertheless, one can't help wondering whether *A. madagascariensis*, or its recent ancestor, survived and flourished here because of the lucky chance that it found hawkmoths in residence and ready to pollinate it, or whether the moths themselves evolved along with the tree.

Nowadays, European bees may also contribute to pollination in places where beekeepers leave hives near Boab trees. Certainly I have seen them, in the early mornings, visiting the flowers of Broome Boabs, all of which have been planted or transplanted from their natural homes.

Other insects, such as ants, which are often found exploring the Boab flowers, probably looking for nectar, are not, as might be thought, pollinating them in return. They crawl down into the floral tube to get to the nectar, but do not come into contact with the reproductive parts of the flower on the way. To contribute to pollination, ants would have to climb up the stamens, carry away a dusting of pollen, and then, because the trees are not normally fertilised by their own pollen, laboriously clamber up a second tree, enter a flower, and make their way up to the stigma, there at last to deposit the pollen from the first tree. No ant is so altruistic.

Having had their day, the flowers turn limp and brown, and a day or so later they drop, first, the brush of spent stamens and, later, their limp, brown petals. Those that have been pollinated successfully leave their pistil behind on the tree, so that the pollen tube can grow inside it and fertilise the ovules. Some days later the ovary swells, and over the next few weeks it develops into the young fruit.

Fully grown but unripe Boab fruits are large, round to ovoid gourd-like

sex, reproduction and death | Chapter 2

Fruiting Boab

objects. Their hard shells are covered with a rich green velvet of fine hairs. As the fruits ripen and age the shells lose their furriness and turn brown and brittle. Some fall to the ground and shatter, revealing the white pith in which the seeds are embedded. Others remain in the tree, sometimes for months, and their shells eventually weather and crack. People wanting to gather intact fruit do so soon after the shells have turned brown, but before they have time to deteriorate in the tree or fall and break.

David Baum points out that this tendency to crack, or functional dehiscence, is not shared by any other species of Baobab. In Chapter One, I discussed the possibility that seeds of the Australian Boab's ancestor travelled to Australia in a buoyant pod and it is clear that such a pod would have had to be thick-walled and tough to survive such an ocean voyage. The shells of all the other species of Baobab are indeed much

opposite: Boab family group on Packsaddle Plains, near Kununurra, WA

sex, reproduction and death   Chapter 2

thicker than that of the Australian species. Tim Willing recalls that on the Kenya coast in the 1950s horizontally split Baobab pods were the standard baler for outrigger canoes, and lasted for years. Boys on the beach practised rugby ball-passing skills with entire pods, which were too hard to kick.

The relatively thinner shells of the Australian nuts certainly evolved here, probably as an aid to seed dispersal by marsupials because there were no powerful mammals such as baboons or lemurs to break them open.

seed dispersal

Boab trees occupy a range of habitats. They commonly follow creek beds and rocky gorges, where nuts and seeds are dispersed by floodwater during the wet. They also favour open woodland or grassland, where they may stand in noble solitude or clustered in groves. In the groves you often

see family groups of trees of different ages, or an almost circular distribution of young trees which must have grown from seeds dropped in the fruit of a deceased parent. A solitary tree is more likely to have grown from a seed transported by an animal, bird or human being.

In gorge country Boab trees are sometimes found in unlikely places, perched high on rocky ledges, so that it is hard at first to understand how they got there after leaving their parent tree. Chris Done of the WA Department of Conservation and Land Management (CALM) answered that question when he discovered viable Boab seeds in the scats of euros and rock wallabies. These animals can climb to places not normally accessible to Boab trees, and they deposit the seeds wherever they move their bowels.

Undoubtedly human beings contributed to the dispersal of Boab trees long before modern times. The seed pods, colloquially known as nuts, are convenient portable containers full of food, and very probably people carried them over considerable distances in order to eat the contents later, or to share them with their families. Though seeds used in cooking would have been destroyed by the processes of grinding and heating, not all were treated in this way. People often ate, and still eat, the raw white pith, spitting out the seeds onto the ground. Some of these ejected seeds would have germinated later and taken root. This sequence of events may account for the presence of Boab trees growing on shell middens here and there along the coast, though it is also possible that some of the middens arose because generations of people sat under a parent Boab's shade while they ate their shellfish.

The seeds of Boab trees have tough skins, and can remain viable for years after ripening. In nature they only germinate in good rainy seasons, conditions which can be simulated in a nursery by providing plenty of water.

When the seeds germinate, the first pair of foliage leaves is simple and heart-shaped, and only the secondary and later leaves are the characteristic compounds with five, six or seven spear-shaped leaflets.

Deciduous trees are able to live in a difficult climate by shedding their leaves and suspending activity during the harshest part of the year. For the Boab this is the long dry season, which usually stretches from March or April to December. The tree's luxuriant burst of foliage at the end of this time is clearly designed to support its fervid reproductive activities and, although the first leaves shoot well before the rain, the subsequent leafing and flowering are invariably supported by some level of seasonal rainfall.

The Boab survives the long dry months by using the water it stores in its tissues during the wet season. The girth of a tree alters measurably from one season to another; the trunk expands with the water it absorbs after rain, and contracts as the stored water is used up during the long dry time. Another unusual adaptation, with obvious value for a leafless tree, is the photosynthetic layer of chlorophyll that covers the bark, just beneath the trunk's outer 'skin'. If you scrape away some of the skin, this dark green layer will be exposed. It is this that makes the trunk slippery to climb when boots have scuffed it. Since photosynthesis is the process by which green plants manufacture food from sunlight, a subcutaneous layer of chlorophyll enables the Boab to supply itself with nutrients throughout the year, even when it has no leaves, albeit then at a reduced rate.

survival

Not only do Boab trees live for a long time, but they are tenacious of life in other respects as well. Trees of most species die if they are ringbarked, but the Boab's bark simply grows back over the wound and repairs it. Its relation, the African Baobab, can tolerate severe damage by elephants, which tear its bark to shreds with their tusks and gouge yawning holes in the tree's trunk. The worst animal damage that Australian Boabs are likely to experience

tenacity

sex, reproduction and death Chapter 2

is having their bark chewed by horses. They are also frequently affected by bush fires. Damage may be little more than a drying and peeling of the outer 'skin', or a loss of the first layer of bark. Severe fires may leave deep scars that expose the soft inner fibre, which may then be further damaged through invasion by fungi and other pests. Fire is probably the primary cause of the hollowing found in certain trunks.

Some big old Boabs become quite hollow, but still they bear foliage and continue to flower and fruit. I have seen one, about eighty kilometres west of Fitzroy Crossing, that has spread so wide and lost so much of its filling that it seems to have forgotten it is a tree. The trunk now consists of a rambling, lumpy wall enclosing space. The interior is open to the skies, and you can peer into it through holes high in the wall. In the bottom of the sunny

PAGE 32

above: Fire damage
opposite: Mulla Mulla (*Ptilotus exaltatus*) and Boabs near Derby, West Kimberley PHOTO: Bill Bachman

sex, reproduction and death | Chapter 2

hollow grow grasses and other plants whose seeds have found their way inside and germinated. Were there only a doorway, you could stable horses in this tree, and not have to worry immediately about supplying them with feed. And still the tree lives.

Boabs that fall down, struck by lightning or toppled in a cyclone because their fibres have rotted and weakened from within, may not die. For another season or longer, even though they have no roots entering the ground, they may put out from their branches fresh green shoots, though they no longer bear flowers and fruit. I have seen more than one fallen Goliath from whose prostrate body have sprung upright branchings with the distinct appearance of new young trees. It has even been said, with some exaggeration, that no one has ever seen a dead Boab. Once these trees do die, their spongy fibrous wood disintegrates remarkably quickly — another reason why dead Boabs are not found lying about the landscape.

While most Boabs grow as a single stem, some divide into two or three or occasionally more stems close to the ground. Rare specimens may look like a hand of bananas. The very biggest Boabs with the greatest girth are formed from double or multiple stems, or perhaps from two or more trees which have spread, pushed against one another, and finally melded together to form a single huge trunk. The forms of the original individual stems are usually still discernible within the agglomerate tree.

stems

Taking all this evidence together, it would appear that the tissue of Boab trees is less specialised than that of most other trees, or perhaps it becomes less so with advancing age. I have seen some gothic specimens with huge horizontal branches that run along the ground, so that at first sight they look like giant roots, almost two metres thick where they leave the tree.

opposite: Boab flower, taken at night

sex, reproduction and death | Chapter 2

That they are branches rather than roots is evident from their terminal foliage. Where the weight of some low branches has brought their extremities in contact with the ground, they have sent up new shoots which appear also to have taken root, and I have wondered whether I was seeing natural cloning taking place.

Another curious phenomenon I have observed occasionally, which suggests poor differentiation of tissue, is the growth of small, adventitious roots from the upper trunk of an old Boab into a long-lasting pool of water trapped in a hollow between the major branches. The water becomes thick with a rich brew of decaying vegetation, and it makes economic sense for the Boab to take advantage of the nutrients offered.

As might be expected of so hardy a tree, young and even mature Boabs are easily transplanted. Their branches and roots can be cut back quite ruthlessly to facilitate transport, and in their new homes the lopped appendages soon regenerate. Boabs like well-drained soils, and are more likely to succumb to excessive watering, which causes stem-rot, than to drought.

All Baobabs are tropical trees. Their natural range falls roughly between the latitudes twenty degrees north and twenty south. Individual members of different species have been grown successfully outside this range, but they cannot tolerate frost. Some specimens of *A. digitata* survived for several years at Kew in England, but a frost finally killed them.

People have been known to bonsai Boab trees. If I could imagine anything sadder than a Baobab freezing to death in an English winter, it would surely be a Boab bound by copper wires, tortured and dwarfed.

opposite: Banana Tree, NT

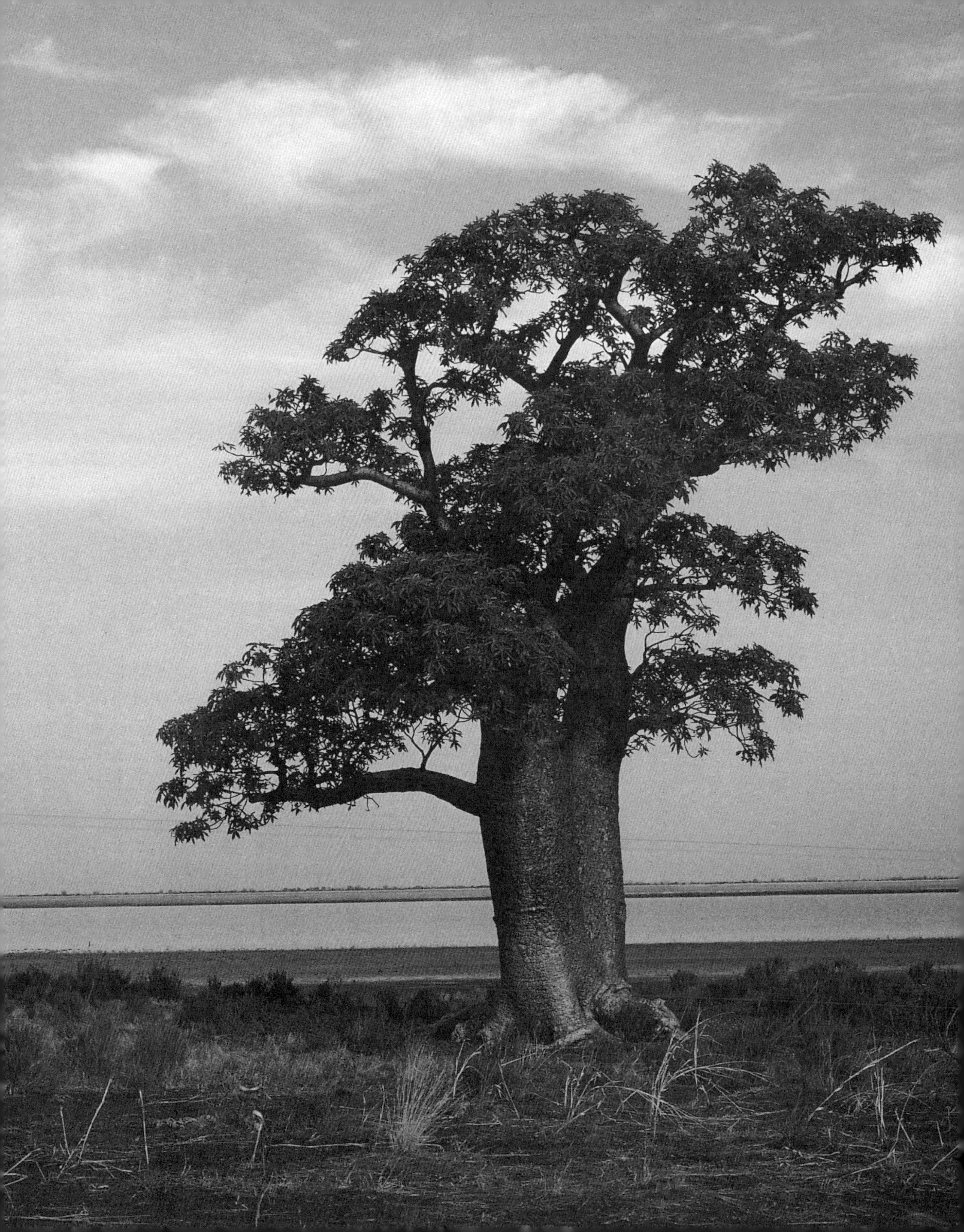

a tree of the people | Chapter 3

Fortunately for the Boab tree's survival, its wood is spongy and fibrous, and of no value as timber. Nevertheless, the tree has been used in numerous ways by the human beings who share its territory.

The Boab tree has a number of indigenous names, a different one for each distinct language group. In Fitzroy Crossing it is usually known by the Bunuba name, *larrkarti*, and the nuts are called *wajarri*. Larrkarti seeds are called *ngipi*. In the Northern Territory around Timber Creek the Ngaliwuru name for the Boab tree is *kuruwan*, and the Nungali name *muruwan*.

names

In leaf, the Boab tree provides deep shade, but even in the dry season, when its branches are bare, the great bulk of an old tree's trunk casts a welcome shadow, except around the middle of the day. Even then, the traveller can usually position himself beneath an overhanging branch until the sun moves lower.

opposite: The Forrest Tree
below: Leopold Downs, Oscar Range, near Fitzroy Crossing, WA

a tree of the people | Chapter 3

water

The tree is valued by the first people of northern Australia as a source of water, and there are different ways in which it serves this need. Some trees are hollow, so that rainwater runs off the leafy canopy and down the branches to collect inside the trunk. This acts as a reservoir to be drawn on in time of drought. We have already seen how old trees become gnarled and pitted. Sometimes the fork between the primary branches develops a shallow cavity which may hold water for a short time after rain. Deeper hollows may form within the scar left by a fallen branch. People passing nearby during the rainy season, knowing this, would make a detour to visit such a tree, and climb as far as the cavity to slake their thirst. During a storm, even smaller holes may collect a cupful of water, which a traveller might come across and enjoy a day or two later.

The Forrest Boab, which we shall meet again in Chapter Five, is a tree with a natural water cavity formed at the point where a branch must once have fallen off. When I visited the tree, a few days after a heavy fall of rain, the cavity was full. Unfortunately, it is quite high off the ground, and one has to chimney up between the tree's two forks to get to the water. Whether that would have been regarded as a convenient source by local Aboriginal people I cannot say, but I imagine they were a lot more lithe than I, who managed to climb level with the cavity and was able to put my hand into the clear water.

I had read, in numerous references, that even in dry weather people could draw upon the water-storing capacity of the Boab's fibrous trunk by making gashes in it with a stone axe or tomahawk and collecting the fluid that drained out. However, Aboriginal people I had spoken to never mentioned getting water in this way. Instead, they always talked about using the water that collected in the hollows of specific known trees. I have tried gashing a tree, and found that the cut, though initially moist, does not drip, and

a tree of the people | Chapter 3

very quickly dries out. Wanting to be sure before I repeated the information I had read, I asked several elderly people, including Daisy Lunganan from Looma, whether they knew anything about cutting the tree to obtain water, and they denied that this was done in their day.

Boab on limestone reef, Oscar Range, near Fitzroy Crossing, WA

a tree of the people — Chapter 3

It is a long time since people led a fully traditional life in the Kimberley and, while a great deal of knowledge and folklore remains, little by little it is getting lost. Nowadays, therefore, not knowing that something was done may not be the same as knowing that it wasn't, and the question of water extraction became for me a minor mystery to be solved. I chased references. I rang up and wrote to authors of articles, asking for their sources, which always seemed to have been other articles or books. I spoke to foresters. And I continued to ask Aboriginal people.

I began to suspect that the story arose through confusion in the literature of the Boab tree with *Brachychiton rupestris*, the Bottle Tree of south-east Queensland, which bears a superficial similarity to the Boab, and is said to produce water under its bark which can be extracted and drunk in an emergency. The Boab in the Kimberley is often called a Bottle Tree, and it is easy to see how the Queensland Bottle Tree's characteristics may have been attributed erroneously to the Boab. Such an error, once published, would be repeated many times.

It was also possible that such an error arose from misunderstandings by investigators of their Aboriginal informants. I came across an example of exactly this. A friend reported that she'd been told by Biddy Simon, the senior woman at Marralam, that people used to obtain water from Boab trees by cutting holes in the trunk. When I pressed my friend for details it turned out that Biddy had merely said, 'We used to get water from Boab trees', and my friend had interpreted this comment according to her own preconceptions, which in turn derived from what she had read. Biddy herself later told me she had not heard of people extracting water from the bark or trunk, but remembered using rainwater stored in hollow trees.

Daisy Lungana of Looma described cutting the trunk, not to extract

a tree of the people Chapter 3

water, but to make what she called a 'ladder', that is, hand- and footholds by which people could climb a tree to reach water held in its hollow. From time to time they cleaned out the debris of sand and blown leaves that collected there, allowing the hollow to be refilled by the next rain.

I had almost convinced myself that all the references were wrong. And then, one day, when I was visiting Derby, I ran into Gordon Barunga, an old acquaintance from Mowanjum. I asked him whether he knew anything about traditional uses of the Boab tree. 'Oh, yes,' he said, casually. 'People used to get water out of the bark.' At last! 'Have you ever done that?' I asked. 'Yes, we used to do it when we were kids.' He was sitting on a bench alongside two much older men, and he turned to them for confirmation. They both nodded agreement. Then Gordon told me how the water extraction was done.

In Gordon Barunga's childhood people used a metal-bladed tomahawk, but in olden times they would have used a stone axe or knife. With this sharp tool they marked out a section of bark, cutting through to the white wood within, and then they loosened and pulled down strips of it. They chewed these strips to extract the moisture, spitting out the fibre when they had sucked it dry. Sometimes, they dug up and chewed the roots of a very young tree instead, which was easier than cutting into a mature Boab's trunk. This would have been an important consideration in the days of stone blades.

The Boab provided people with food in several forms, of which the best known is found within the pod or nut. The ripe nut is filled with a dry, brittle, powdery white pith, the texture of styrofoam, in which the seeds are embedded. The pith, though mouth-drying and flavourless at first bite, contains vitamin C and tastes acidic when chewed. People eat it as it comes out of the shell, or crush it up with water and drink the wet pulp like a cordial. In earlier times they used to sweeten the liquid with the honey of native bees,

food

a tree of the people | Chapter 3

more recently with sugar. Connoisseurs of Boab nuts tell me that the nut contents vary considerably in sweetness of taste. Now that carbonated drinks have become so readily available, they have almost entirely replaced this wholesome natural beverage in popularity, and many young local people have never so much as sampled juice made from the pith of the Boab nut.

While the pith from the ripe nuts whose shells have turned brown may be extracted and eaten raw, the green nuts may also be eaten, either raw or cooked. Unripe nuts are picked from still-leafy trees, and baked in the ground with hot coals. After about half an hour they are ready to open and eat.

During the North Australian Exploring Expedition led by Augustus Gregory, members of the expedition team and the crew of their schooner the

a tree of the people | Chapter 3

Tom Tough became ill with scurvy. It was Thomas Baines, the expedition's artist and storeman, who discovered the curative properties of the pith of the Boab nut, which he boiled with sugar and made into 'an agreeable jam', as the expedition geologist Wilson describes it in his journal. According to Baines, within a few short weeks of adding the Boab fruit pulp to their diet, the scurvy sufferers had fully recovered.

Explorer Herbert Basedow, who visited the Kimberley in 1916, describes children 'shying toy boomerangs and pieces of bark' at ripening nuts, in an effort to knock them out of a tree. He also mentions that 'bushmen often add some of the mucilaginous pulp to the flour when making damper; it is said to be a good substitute for baking powder'. The pulp contains tartaric acid.

People also used the seeds of the Boab tree as a food. These they ground into a paste, which they ate raw. This process is hard and lengthy work, and no one seems to do it any more, except perhaps as a demonstration of traditional practices. Sometimes the seeds were roasted in the coals and eaten whole. They contain protein and oil.

The leaves are a nutritious green vegetable, but should be eaten at their best, when young and fresh. Fully developed leaves have a slightly bitter taste. Boab leaves have also been used as emergency feed for cattle.

Many trees of Australia, notably Eucalyptus and Owenia, exude a coloured resin when their bark is injured. The resin of the eucalypts has medicinal properties; that of the Turtujarti (*Owenia reticulata*) is edible, and people used to cut a tree's bark in several places in order to make it form blobs of resin.

It is said that the Boab tree also produces an edible resin when the wood is injured, but I have never seen it. Tim Willing has seen it occasionally,

opposite: The honey tree, Oscar Range, near Fitzroy Crossing, WA

but only on trees that have been severely injured, and conjectures that the gum is produced when the injury penetrates through the thickness of the bark to the internal wood. I once saw a brown, gummy substance in the rotting wound left after one stem of an old Boab had fallen, but the stench was such that eating the gum would have been unthinkable. In any case, the gum is exuded rarely enough for it to have been an occasional delicacy rather than an important part of the local people's diet.

Even the roots of the young tree are edible. They are relatively shallow and can be unearthed and exposed quite easily. The taproot of a very young tree is cut and a segment removed. This surgery does not seem to harm the tree provided it is left in place and not uprooted altogether. Roots of even smaller trees may be eaten whole. With the bark peeled off, the young root is edible raw or lightly cooked in the coals, and has the texture of a carrot. In the past, people would collect enough young roots to feed their families.

traditional uses

Products of the Boab were put to other uses besides being eaten. People used the tree's fibres for making cord. They would cut the root, strip the fibre and arrange it in suitable lengths. Then, sitting on the ground, they would rub it back and forth against the thigh to make the fibres bind together. Old people from Kalumburu learned to make cord like this when they were young, and it was an elderly woman named Manuela Burrwan who demonstrated the method to me when I visited her community several years ago.

I hoped to return to Kalumburu to learn more about local uses of the Boab tree. I particularly wanted to talk to Mary Pandilo, one of the oldest members of that community with a wealth of traditional knowledge, who had been absent during my previous visit. But several years went by and the opportunity to go back there never came.

opposite: Warmun (Turkey Creek), East Kimberley, WA

a tree of the people Chapter 3

Then one day at sunset, on the Gibb River Road, when I was on my way to Mornington Station and had pulled in at Imintji for fuel, a dusty Landcruiser turned up, travelling in the opposite direction. Out stepped the familiar figures of Dennis and Margaret Howard, on their way from Kalumburu to Broome. With them in the car was Mary Pandilo.

It was hardly the time to talk about Boab trees, but as a result of that brief encounter I later called Dennis and explained to him what I needed. He passed my request on to Margaret, who was working as a linguist at Kalumburu, and she and Mary recorded for me a conversation about the subject nearest to my heart.

a tree of the people | Chapter 3

In that recording Mary, a Gwini woman whose language is Guniin, added new information to that I had already gathered. She told how people used to climb Boab trees, called *jumulu* in Mary's language, to pull down young, green nuts to cook in the fire. She talked of picking up dry nuts from the ground, smashing the pith with a stone, and then soaking it in water with honey to make a drink.

Mary explained that fibre for cord was obtained from the bark of the Boab as well as from its roots: 'They make the string out of the bark, from on top, where they cut it with a axe or a stone – they didn't have axe before – with a stone.' The strips of fibre were then pounded with a rock to 'make them like wool', which could then be rolled against the thigh into a long string or thicker rope. The string is called *bii*.

The string or rope served many purposes, as did hair string in other parts of Australia. It was used as a shoulder strap for a cradle or dish of bark, similar to a coolamon and known as a *warnda* in Mary's language, in which babies were carried. The bark is pleated and tied at each end, again with Boab string. Mary herself had been carried in this way: 'When we were babies, they make the big string to carry us ... carrying us with the *warnda*, if you know what is the *warnda*, the coolamon.' Women also carried *warnda* on their heads or suspended from their shoulders with Boab string to transport food they gathered.

Thicker rope was strong enough to tie up a canoe: 'When they have canoe they can make the string for it ... like a rope, to hold the canoe there. They tie im up with that Boab tree rope, into the mangrove tree, and then he hold the canoe. He won't run away from them.'

Packages made of paperbark, *marimbu* in Guniin, and tied with Boab tree string were used to store food, including pulp soaked in honey water.

opposite: Gregory National Park, NT

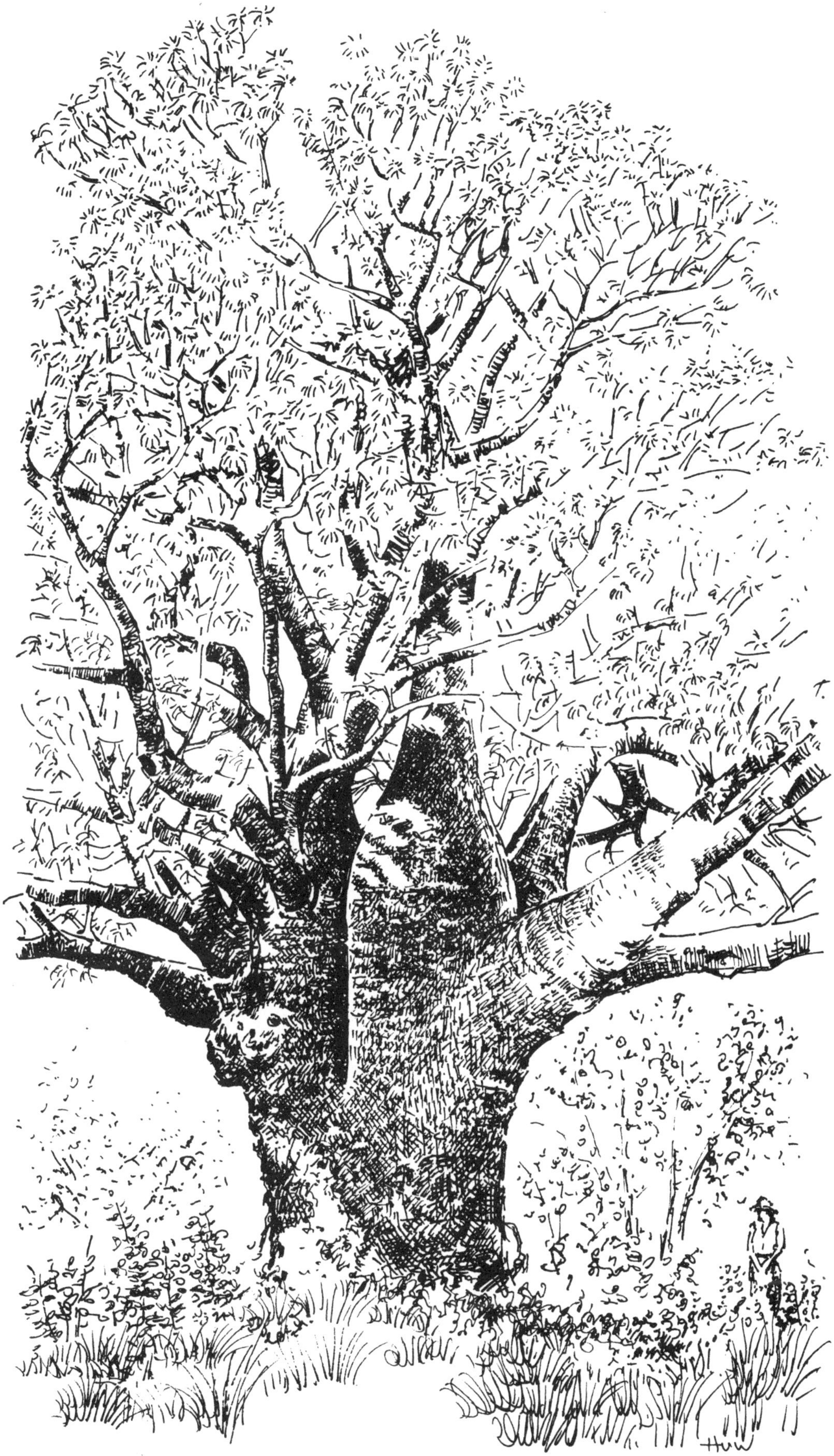

a tree of the people · Chapter 3

Mary drew an analogy between the paperbark packages of her childhood and a modern eski, which serves a similar function.

Both men and women used *bii* around their hair. 'They put it in their hair, like a ribbon.'

Boab tree string is also used to make ceremonial crosses. The string is woven across the four arms of a stick cross to form a sort of tapestry or mat. A man carries such a cross and men and women follow him in dance formation.

Like Biddy Simon from Marralam, Mary Pandilo described climbing old trees to find water in the hollows between the main branches, adding the detail that people scooped it out with a baler shell. Kalumburu is on the coast, where baler shells are plentiful and in the old days were used as drinking vessels. People living further from the coast, in Bunuba country for example, used containers like small coolamons, carved from wood, or perhaps even broken Boab nut shells.

dangers Travellers of every generation, whether locals or newcomers, have been glad to rest in the Boab tree's shade during the heat of the day. 'But not in the night time,' warns Mary. It is dangerous to sleep under a Boab tree. 'Especially rain time, the snake stop on top too, yeah. And they can fall on top of you.'

Neither do people burn the wood in their cooking fires. It is true that dry Boab wood is light and spongy, burns up quickly and doesn't leave good embers. However, as a child Mary was warned that burning it could also 'make you light; all your body will be light' like the wood itself. On the other hand, people lay green leaves in their fire to make smoke which keeps mosquitoes at bay. A leafy branch can also be used as a bed on which to place cooked meat or fish when it is pulled from the ground oven: 'like a plate, you know?'

opposite: Twin Boab trees, near Fig Tree Yard, Gregory National Park PHOTO: Bill Bachman

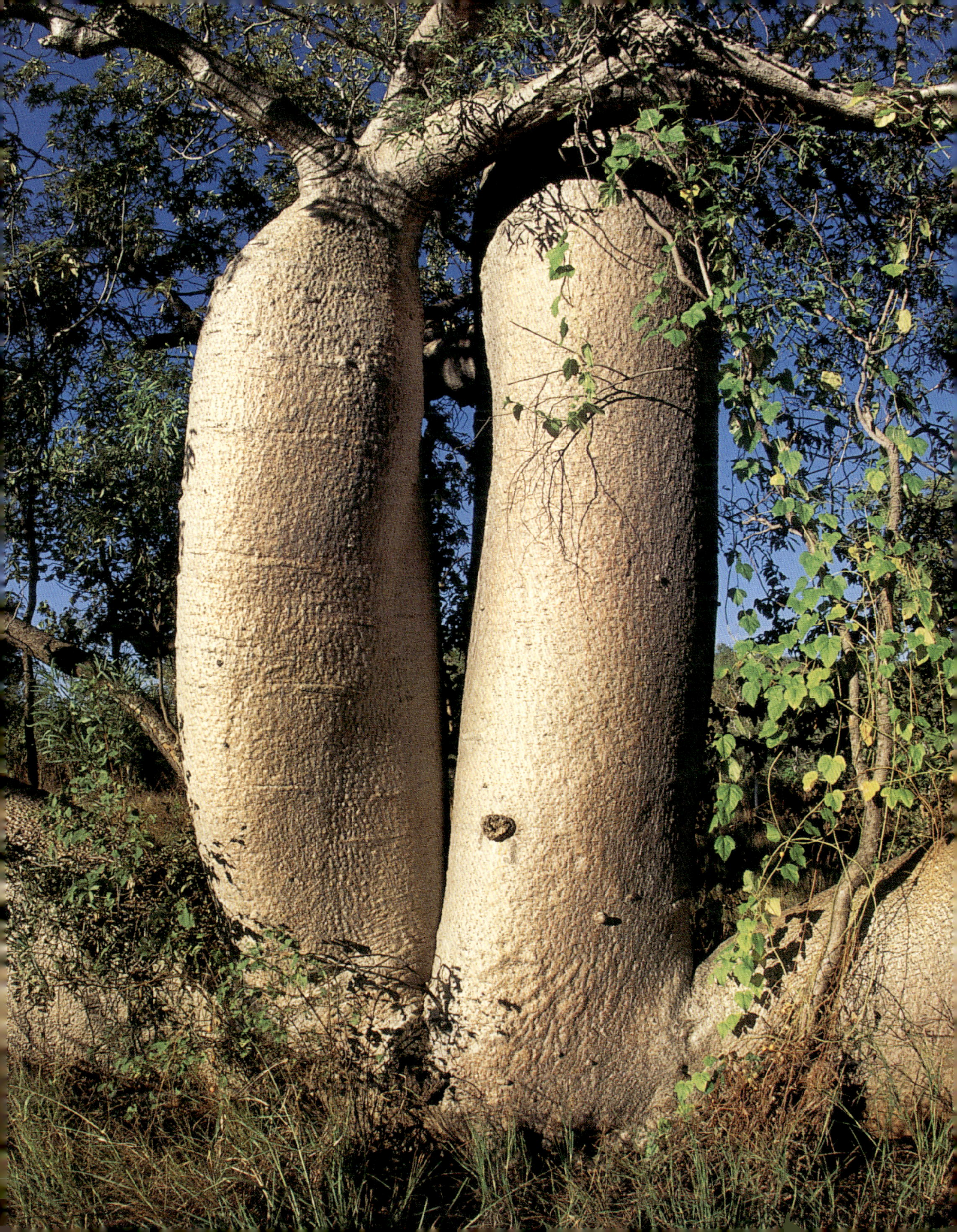

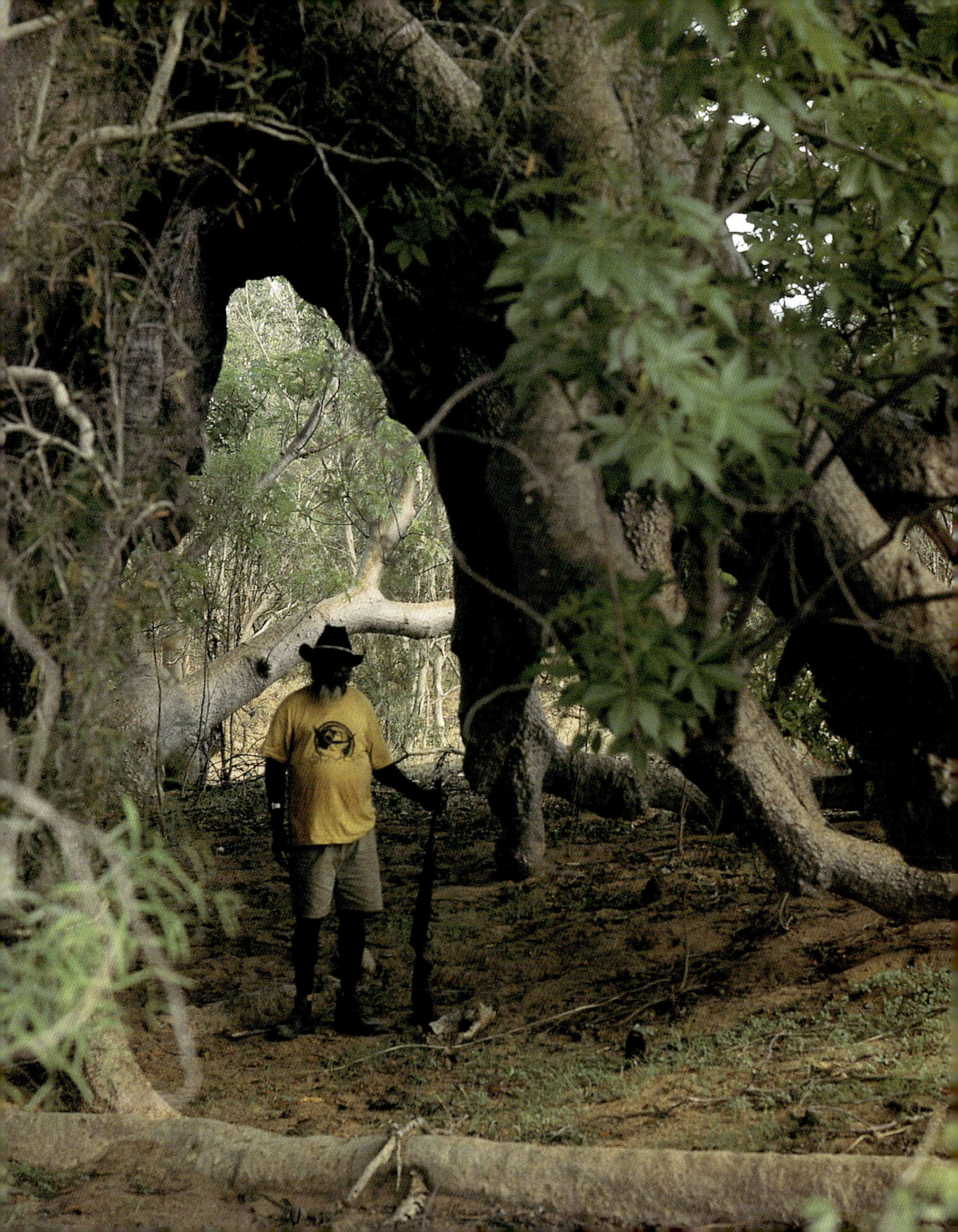

a tree of the people | Chapter 3

Not surprisingly in view of their association with water, certain Boab trees have an influence on rainfall. Mary Pandilo says that a particular tree in *Olngorru*, which is Mary's spirit country in Berkeley Plain, has this power: 'The special Boab tree, if you touch it, like in *Olngorru* you know, they can make rain. If you hit or touch the tree, even if you sit underneath it, he can make you rain.'

top: Carved Boab nuts
bottom: The Gravel Pit, Oscar Range, WA
opposite: Massive Boab branches bent to the ground under their own weight, near the Logue River, West Kimberley

a tree of the people | Chapter 3

carved nuts

Nowadays, ripe Boab nuts are more in demand for carving into ornaments than as a food. Because the brittle shells break on impact with the ground, nuts for carving have to be picked from the tree when they are mature and brown. Local people carve intricate pictures over their surface, using a pocket knife, and sell them to tourists, or to shops catering to such. Some of the best carved Boab nuts are works of art, depicting wildlife in the bush, or hunting scenes, or human faces and figures. Most artists prefer to work on large nuts, which give them greater artistic scope and usually fetch a higher price, but some favour very small ones, which they carve to look like whole birds or echidnas.

A west Kimberley myth concerns Larrkarti, the lecherous anthropomorphic tree figure who travelled through the Kimberley in the creation time. His exploits are recorded in the form of a particular Boab tree, familiar to local people. It immortalises the enormous erection he produced at the sight of four girls whose path he crossed. He chased them through the bush. This tree stands not far off the Looma road. Unfortunately, someone in recent years has taken to Larrkarti's phallus with an axe. It is now not only foreshortened, but scarred along the still substantial remains of its shaft.

Boab trees embody dangerous powers. Someone intending to harm another person used to draw an effigy of his victim in the bark of a Boab trunk, name it, and then sing a malevolent song. As a result of this bad magic, the victim, usually a person who had broken a taboo, would blow up 'like a balloon', or like a Boab tree.

It is inadvisable to break off a flowering branch. To do so is to invite a powerful wind, with rain and lightning, which will seek out the offender in revenge for the flower destroyed.

In southern Africa there is a myth, whose details vary in the retelling,

a tree of the people | Chapter 3

that around the time of its creation the Baobab tree was uprooted and replanted upside-down. This fate explains its strange appearance during the dry season, when its leafless branches assume weird shapes and look like exposed roots. Non-indigenous Kimberley residents sometimes confidently relate a variation on this tale as an Aboriginal creation myth about the Boab tree, but they may have their countries, and their trees, confused.

As one might expect, the Boab tree features in traditional stories of the Kimberley and Northern Territory. In the book *Joe Nangan's Dreaming* there is a story about the giant Wedge-tailed Eagle who preyed on infant human beings and terrorised the people of several language groups. This eagle had her nest in a Boab tree. Eventually she was defeated and killed by two boys, who also broke her egg to prevent her from reproducing. The boys later became the owl and the sandbird.

A Northern Territory story retold by Anne Carmel Mulvien from Daly River tells how two brolgas sucked all the water from the rivers, creeks, waterholes and billabongs, and put it into a Boab tree. The other animals went looking for the water, and the sand frog found it in the tree. He threw a spear which pierced the tree's trunk and the water rushed out and refilled the creeks. All the animals rejoiced.

stories

the familiar | Chapter 4

The place in the Kimberley most closely associated in people's minds with the Boab tree is Derby. This little town on the mudflats of King Sound derives much of its character from the individualistic gnarled old Boabs that preside over its streets. One night some years ago an esteemed ancient tree that had always stood outside Rusty's general store tottered and fell, plunging the residents into mourning. Almost as well known is the Love Tree at Colac Roadhouse: really two trees, a Boab and a white gum so entwined that they have become as one, like a devoted married couple.

Because of their ubiquity in Derby, Boabs have become a tourist icon. The tree is featured, with greater or lesser artistic merit, on postcards, tea towels, keyrings and in glass-encapsulated snowstorms. The town hosts an annual Boab Festival in the dry season with events that include a country and western night, a rodeo and, for the less heroic, mud crab races.

It is from the country north of Derby that the tree appears to have dispersed inland. From the perspective of a traveller heading north and east from Broome, the naturally propagated Boabs begin quite suddenly near the 110-kilometre mark halfway between the two towns, just beyond Nillibubbica.

A few stray Boabs can be found by the careful observer in the bush closer to Broome. One group of three immature young trees stands near a former cattle yard about forty kilometres out. There is no other Boab for miles from which these infants could have sprung; they must therefore have been transported over a considerable distance as seeds. Since an animal is unlikely to have travelled seventy kilometres before depositing the seeds in its droppings, human beings are the more probable agents of dispersal in this case. Given the youthfulness of the three trees, a possible scenario is of people travelling by horse or by car and carrying with them some of the seed pods,

opposite: Boab at dawn, early wet season, near Logue River, West Kimberley, WA

which they opened in that place in order to eat the pithy contents. The discarded seeds would have lain where they fell until they germinated during a season of good rain. More prosaically, they may have been planted.

A solitary mature tree, of considerable girth, can be found about seventy kilometres from Broome, near some artificial dams left by gravel mining. It is a splendid specimen, with a stout, straight trunk constricting near the top, and a symmetrical crown.

Within Broome itself a number of Boab trees can be found in unusual and even inexplicable places. One small specimen occupies an obscure but enviable position on top of a dune behind the old meatworks site, transplanted there, as the regrowth of its limbs from severed stumps betrays, by persons and for reasons unknown. Another, thought to have been planted long ago by Patrick Percy, the former Lighthouse keeper, still stands out on the promontory at Ganthéaume Point. Short, stunted and gnarled, this tree has been shaped by the prevailing ocean winds, and has attracted the interest of many artists and photographers. Its crown has been swept to one side like a head of hair in the wind. Home for numerous bagmoths and a solitary perch for birds, this valiant little tree stands dwarfed by the lighthouse behind it. Year after year, too exposed to the elements to hold more than a few flowers, and too far from others of its kind to be cross-pollinated, it bears no fruit.

One or two young strays have found their way to the open country near Crab Creek, perhaps relations of the planted population in Broome.

From Derby the trees radiate north and east the width of the Kimberley, crossing the border into the Northern Territory, where they have spread by random means along the Victoria River. The traveller need not move far from the road to find interesting specimens. The Gibb River Road is particularly rich in them, as is the highway between Kununurra and Timber Creek. In the Oscar Range Boab trees enhance the rocky landscape. As in Broome, Boabs have been cultivated successfully in both Katherine and Darwin.

Australian Boabs are also growing in other parts of the world. Max Clarke, who has lived in Derby for many years, tells me that there was once a thriving export industry. Adult Boabs from the bush, their roots and branches severely lopped, were trucked to the Derby wharf and shipped to foreign destinations. Nowadays, the trees are protected from such exploitation, and during the 1980s there was an outcry when the Logue River grove was similarly plundered of its trees to line the streets of Broome.

People who have spent all their lives in Boab country, or who have lived there for a long time, know particular trees along the roadsides, at which they make a habit of stopping for a break in their journeys. Between Derby and Fitzroy Crossing, several such trees catch the eye and often induce the traveller to pull up for a rest in their generous shade. One of these, a hollow specimen with a girth of seventeen metres, standing some sixty-five kilometres from the Derby–Fitzroy turn-off, has been staked out by the Derby Shire and surrounded with a low log fence. When the fence first appeared, I marvelled that anyone would go to such trouble to no apparent purpose, particularly as the fence hinders the parking of cars close enough to the tree to benefit from its shade. I have since concluded that such hindrance *is* the fence's purpose — to prevent people from parking under a large, heavy horizontal branch, which might conceivably decide one day, without warning, to break off and fall on any car unfortunate enough to be parked below. More recently, the site has been embellished by the arrival of two fixed tables with benches for picnickers who eschew the earth as a place to sit.

the familiar | Chapter 4

Another tree is the stopping place for drivers in a hurry who want to make just one pit-stop on their way from Broome or Derby to Fitzroy Crossing. This Half-way Tree is eighty-six kilometres from the turn-off, on the right-hand side for people heading east. I am told by Gwen Knox, who grew up in the Kimberley, that the original Half-way Tree used to grow on the opposite side of the road, and that the present one so known was in those days the Toilet Tree. At length, in the late 1970s, the Half-way Tree died, full of wisdom and years, leaving the well-fertilised Toilet Tree to assume its superior role. The last time I stopped at that tree, I was dismayed to notice that it now serves a dual function.

About ninety kilometres west of Fitzroy Crossing, on the left-hand side as you approach, lies an artificial billabong which fills up with water during the Wet, and where brolgas and Brahmin cattle gather on the bank. A track leads into the water from the road, and travellers like myself who know the spot often stop there on a hot day to refresh themselves and their dogs. An old and thick-stemmed Boab tree stands by the track. Until quite recently it had two trunks, and was a generous provider of shade. One day, a few years ago, on my way to Fitzroy Crossing, I parked in that shade while I walked down to the edge of the billabong, and my dogs plunged into the water. Less than a week later, on my way back to Broome, I was saddened to find that one fork of the tree's great trunk had fallen down, and lay like a defeated giant across the track. As I approached, a powerful but not disgusting smell of rot met me. Where the fallen trunk had split away from its still standing companion, the enormous wound revealed a damp, rotting, mucilaginous fibrous mass. The tree must have been decaying from within, and had needed only a strong wind to separate it at the joint.

When next I visited the same billabong, only a few months later, I was surprised to find that all trace of the smell and rot had disappeared. The fibrous wound had dried out. What's more, the fallen trunk, far from having died, had continued to behave as if it were still firmly planted in the earth. It had fallen when in leaf; thereafter, in my absence, it must have flowered, for on my return it was bearing mature nuts. They were easily within my reach, and I picked some of them.

opposite: Mount Anderson, near Looma, West Kimberley, WA

The following year the branches sprouted fresh leaves again, but some time later than did the ones on the still standing trunk. The tree bore no flowers, and no nuts grew.

One of the best known Kimberley Boabs is the Derby Prison Tree. This is a huge, hollow Boab a short way off the road just out of town. The shell of the trunk is almost spherical, and the space within big enough to accommodate several people, standing, sitting or even lying down, and there is a door-sized entrance. It is said that, in the days when Aboriginal prisoners captured in the bush were put in chains and made to walk the many miles to court, this tree was used as a camping place in which they were kept overnight. Since prisoners were chained together, and had camped in the scrub for many a night before they were brought thus far, there seems to have been little reason to shut them up when they reached the hollow tree. If the tree was used as a stage on the journey, I imagine that the prisoners would have sat in the tree's shade during the day, and used its interior as shelter from rain or from dry season night-time cold. We are not told where their captors sheltered, but there is today a Boab Hotel in Derby town. Local Aboriginal people say that prisoners were never kept inside the tree, but were chained around it in the shade.

Anthropologist Kim Akerman tells me that there is no record of the so-called Prison Tree ever having been used as a lock-up. He points out that, with Derby so close, the policemen captors would have pressed on to the town rather than spend an unnecessary additional night in the scrub. Certainly Basedow, who visited the tree on his 1916 expedition, makes no mention of it being used by police. He said, 'The natives have long been in the habit of making use of this *lusus naturae** as a habitation; it is indeed a dry and comfortable hut' (not so dry during the wet time — the 'roof' gapes

*freak of nature

the familiar | Chapter 4

open to the sky). He found 'bleached human bones ... lying on the floor, which suggested that the tribe had also made use of the tree for disposing of the dead'. There was a bullet hole through one of the skulls Basedow found there.

Many Aboriginal groups share the custom of avoiding any tangible reminder of dead people, including modern artefacts such as photographs and recordings, and I found it hard to imagine them sheltering in the same tree they used as a mortuary.

Alice Downs, near Purnululu, East Kimberley, WA

the familiar | Chapter 4

Basedow saw the bones, I reasoned, but he did not say he witnessed people using the tree 'as a habitation', and I wondered whether he was simply repeating a local myth, just as the Prison Tree myth is repeated nowadays. This tree, with its great interior space and natural entrance, looks as if it *ought* to be inhabited, but it may never have housed anyone but ghosts.

I raised my doubts with Kim Akerman, who did not see any contradiction in the same place serving as both shelter and morgue. He explained that 'most cave and rock shelter living spaces were also used as repositories for bones, and provided the mortuary rites were properly conducted the bones at the conclusion of ceremonies were perceived to be only bones'. He also remarked that 'bones of strangers were treated very off-handedly', and he once observed children at a community 'playing football with a skull'.

Indeed Basedow, later in his own account, describes how his Aboriginal companion Bandignan retrieved a skull from its position on a perilous rock face: 'Bandignan skilfully clambered up the cliff to where the cranium had been planted. Without any sign of repugnance he handed it to me.'

In contrast to the Derby Prison Tree, there are records of the Wyndham Prison Tree having been used as a temporary lock-up.

Aboriginal people have unhappy memories and stories associated with other trees as well. Near Fitzroy Crossing is a Boab tree where people were chained up when they were arrested for killing cattle on what they considered their lands. Stumpy Brown remembers as a child being with a group of her own family members when they were captured by police and kept chained together by the neck around that tree.

Senior Nyikina man, John Watson, told me of a tree near Mount Anderson Station that people call 'Tragedy'. Once, a man named Darcy Ryder

the familiar | Chapter 4

Tragedy Tree

travelled along the road past the station, which was then the main highway between Derby and Fitzroy Crossing. He was on his way to Derby when he met a couple he knew travelling in the opposite direction. It was late in the day, so the three people stopped to camp where they were, near an old Boab tree. One of the men produced a bottle of rum, and they started yarning by the camp fire, taking swigs at the bottle and passing it round. Finally, the rum was gone and Darcy went to his swag to sleep. A short time later he heard raised voices, then the sound of blows. He realised that the other man and his wife were fighting. He lay there for a while, and perhaps he remonstrated with the couple. Soon it was clear that the woman was getting the worst of the fight. Darcy got up from his swag and entered the fray to defend the woman from injury. He gave his friend a hiding and knocked him down. The man never got up again; he was dead.

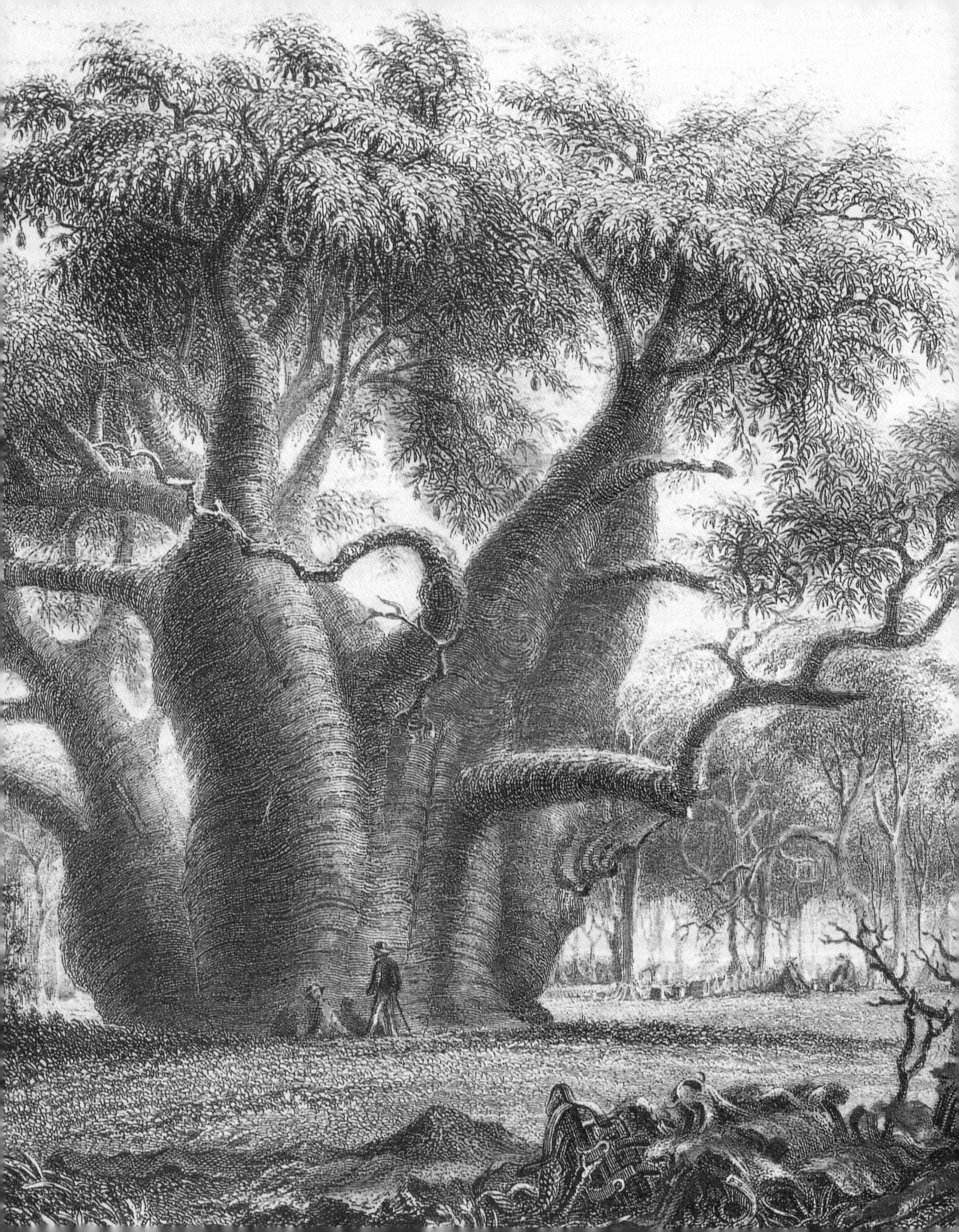

the famous | Chapter 5

Allusions to the Gouty-stem Tree can be found in ships' records and botanical literature from the earliest days of European exploration of the northern coast of Australia:

> There was a very remarkable feature in the appearance of this part of the country, caused by a number of gouty stemmed trees (a species of Caparis [sic]?).
> — Grey G., 1840, *North-west & Western Australia*. Vols 1 & 2.

Some explorers were not above carving their own or their ships' names or initials into the trunks of large specimens, much as thoughtless or egotistical tourists do today. Venerability and fame have, of course, endowed these old signatures with a historical significance that passing tourists can never hope to emulate. Most of them have also been inscribed with a draftsman's skill. One example is the Mermaid tree still standing at Careening Bay on the Kimberley coast, on whose trunk the crew of HMC *Mermaid*, under the command of Phillip Parker King, carved their ship's name in large letters, with the year of its visit there, 1820.*

the Mermaid tree

* *Some authorities see a ghostly 'B' next to the 'H' to read 'His Britannic Majesty's Cutter'.*

PAGE 63

opposite: 'The Boab Tree' by Thomas Baines, official artist for Augustus Gregory's North Australian Exploring Expedition, 1855–6, steel engraving from Edwin C. Boothe's *Australia*, Vol. II, (London, 1876). *courtesy of Durack Gallery, Broome, WA*

the famous | Chapter 5

The *Mermaid* was carrying out a hydrographic survey of the Kimberley coast when it started leaking badly, and King was forced to look for a place to careen the cutter and carry out substantial repairs. He found an ideal bay with a beach at which to do this, and named it after the task at hand. In accordance with Admiralty instructions to 'take care to leave some evidence which cannot be mistaken of your having landed' wherever he did so, King had the ship's name deeply engraved across the double trunk of a nearby massive gouty-stemmed tree. Allan Cunningham, the expedition's botanist, was the

above: Panton River, East Kimberley, WA
opposite: Termite mound and Boab tree, along East Baines River, Gregory National Park, NT
PHOTO: Bill Bachman

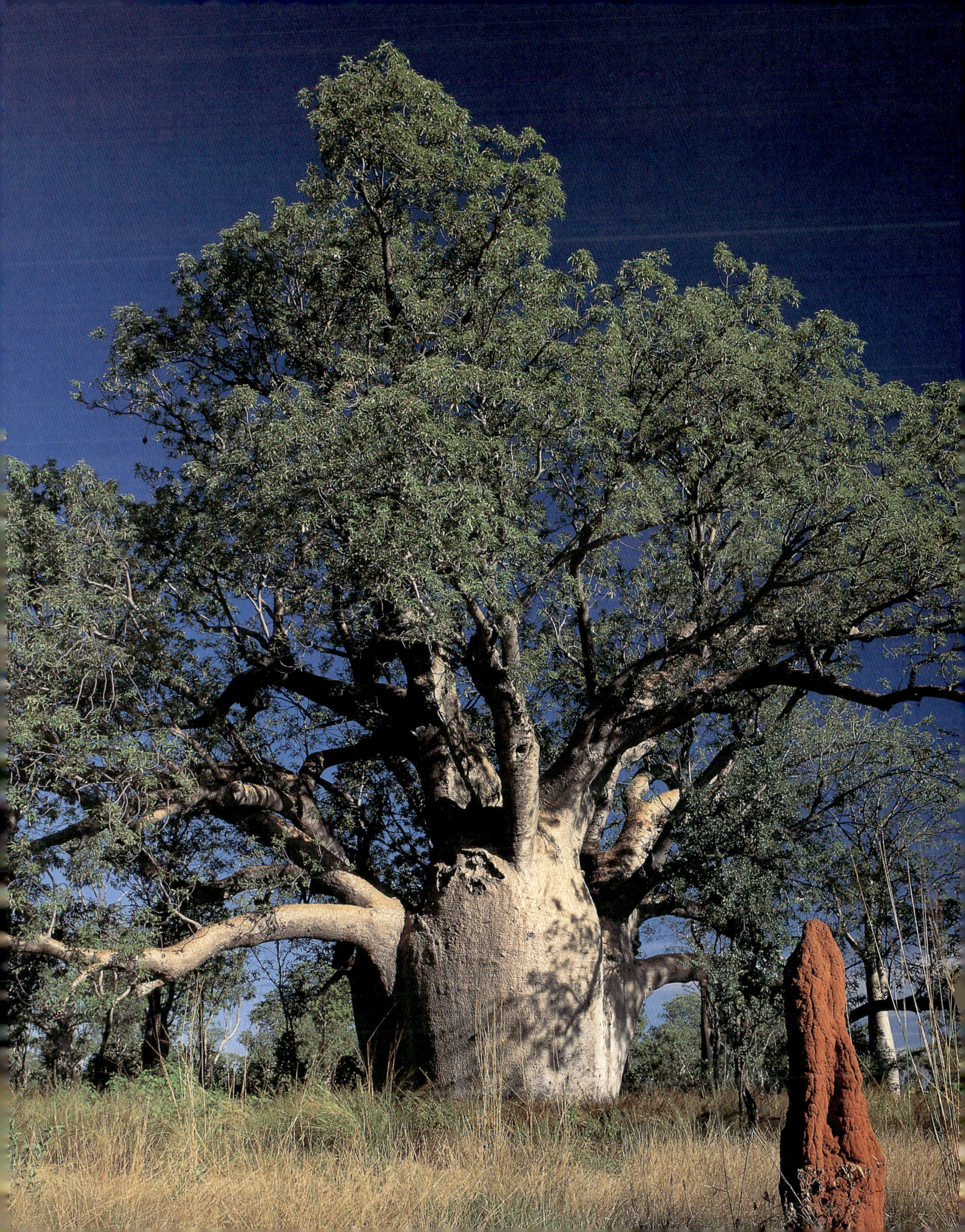

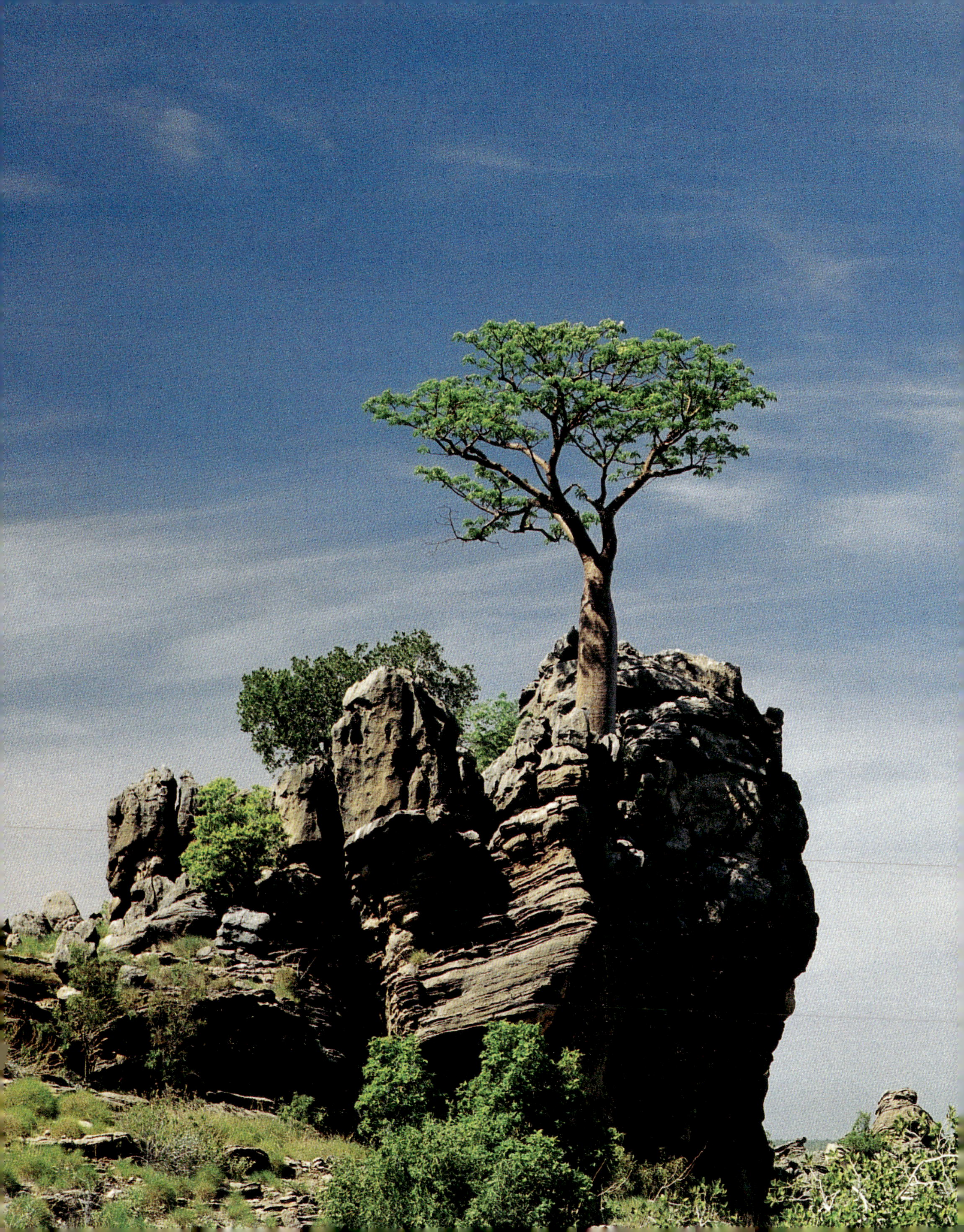

first European to describe this species, which he believed to be a Capparis. Cunningham noted that, as well as on the tree, the name of the vessel was 'more endurably punched onto a sheet of copper which was fastened on the stem of a Hibiscus Tiliacus [sic] growing on the beach'. He could hardly have imagined that the inscription on the tree would endure into the next millennium. I do not know what became of the sheet of copper, but as Tim Willing has pointed out, local Aborigines or visiting Macassans would have found it irresistible.*

In 1820, according to Cunningham, the tree's girth measured 29 feet, or 8.8 metres. Nearly a hundred and eighty years later it measures 12.2 metres. The inscription, spread across two stems, today forms an obtuse angle. Assuming, as seems most likely, that the original lettering was composed in a straight line, the angle formed by the two parts is a measure of the degree to which the stems have since pushed one another outwards and tilted sideways as they thickened. The increase in circumference of each stem has also widened the individual letters, giving them a stretched appearance. Distinct footholds are still discernible in the upper section of the tree, probably cut by King's crew who may have used the tree as a lookout against possible ambush by local people or Macassan pirates.

Macassan fishermen, who engaged in piracy as a sideline, were already frequent visitors to the north Australian coast, where they fished for trepang, an edible sea-slug also known as *bêche-de-mer*. They would have put into the same bay and taken water on board their prahus at the same stream from which King replenished *Mermaid*. Cut deeply into the opposite side of the tree from the *Mermaid*'s name is an alcove which Tim Willing believes to be an Islamic mihrab or prayer niche. It was probably made by Macassans some time after 1820, since neither King nor Cunningham mentions it in his

* Macassar is a seaport on the Celebes islands of the Malay archipelago.

opposite: Boab growing on limestone rocks in the Oscar Range, near Fitzroy Crossing, WA. Boab seeds are deposited in such unlikely places by euros and rock wallabies. PHOTO: Gill Burt

the famous | Chapter 5

journal. Above the niche are cryptic marks that could be faded Arabic lettering.

Forrest Tree

Another historical tree which I have been privileged to visit was inscribed by Alexander Forrest during his Kimberley expedition of 1879 (see photograph on page 36). The tree was rediscovered by Dr Peasley and others on their 1979 centenary ex-pedition which retraced Forrest's steps. When I went to search for the tree with my friends, Tim Willing and Alison Spencer, on Boxing Day 1994, we were excited to find it in good shape with its inscriptions still distinct. This tree has twin trunks which, when in leaf, together provide substantial shade. Besides the well-known 'F' above the number '69' on the eastern side of the tree, marking the expedition's sixty-ninth camp, and the 'H' for Arthur Hicks or Fenton Hill, both members of the same expedition, on the western side, we found a number of less distinct markings, including a second '69' carved obliquely underneath the first. We celebrated our find with a billy of tea and a piece of gourmet fruit cake.

Basedow expedition

Herbert Basedow led a mineralogical expedition to the Kimberley in 1916. The purpose of his exploration was to help supply Britain with materials for manufacturing munitions as part of the Australian war effort. In his entertaining report Basedow describes a number of Baobab trees, as they were still called, and was particularly excited to find one 'with the name "STOKES", carved in capitals deeply into its bark'. The inscription 'could refer to none other than to that distinguished navigator Commander John Lort Stokes, R.N., who in 1838 visited King Sound and named the Fitzroy River'.

Stokes was a naval surveyor who joined HMS *Beagle* as a Midshipman and accompanied Darwin on the *Beagle*'s famous expedition to Australia. He spent eighteen years with the same ship and worked his way up the ranks to become its Commander. He conducted overland as well as marine exploration, as the engraving on the tree discovered by Basedow testifies.

In 1997 I drove to Meda Station with a map, hoping to find the tree described by Basedow, but the station manager told me he had ridden all through the relevant stand of trees looking for it without success. He believed that either the tree had died or the bark, along with the inscription, had been eaten by stock. Ian Obern, who is also familiar with that stand of trees, agrees that the Stokes inscription, if not the tree itself, has disappeared.

Basedow also mentioned two trees on Meda Station bearing Aboriginal markings. One carving of emu tracks he removed with the bark and deposited in the Australian Museum. The others he found on a 'spreading baobab tree opposite Emmanuel Yard':

> Near the base of the massive butt of the tree we were under, several designs had been carved into the bark by native hand. Among other less obvious figures we recognised an emu three feet high, an emu track and a snake, five feet in length. The carvings are well executed; the toes of the bird are shown in plan, and the head of the serpent is especially clear.

I found what I am convinced is this same tree near the now derelict old Emmanuel Yard, where only the weathered timbers remain. It stands distinguished by age and size from all the other members of its species scattered around the yard and along the creek on the other side. Yet the tree bears no evidence of the carvings described by Basedow. However, sections of the bark have clearly been removed from the trunk, and it may be that Basedow, or a subsequent visitor, vandalised this tree for souvenirs as well.

Old reports and I. M. Crawford in his book, *The Art of the Wandjina*, suggest that Boab trees bearing Aboriginal carvings used to be common, but damage by fire, livestock and human visitors as well as natural attrition

the famous | Chapter 5

seems to have reduced their number severely. Nevertheless, such trees may still be discovered by the assiduous searcher. A tree on the Hann River, near Mount Barnett, depicts a human figure on one side and wallaby tracks on the other. These markings are 'public', and may be viewed by anyone. Some marked trees hold secrets, to be understood only by people with certain knowledge and status. There are trees special to senior women or senior men, according to the stories associated with them.

Crawford described several examples of trees in the East Kimberley, on Karunjie Station and near Wyndham, whose markings remain intact thirty years later. Crawford also noted:

> The trees provide shade from the sun, and under each tree one can find a slab of stone on which to break up the nuts of the tree, and a scatter of chips of stone, the waste material from the manufacture of spear heads.

Nowadays most of the stone slabs have disappeared, but scatterings of worked glass and quartz can also occasionally still be found at the foot of Boab trees. Spearhead makers used to cache their materials and half-made pieces amongst the roots of the trees that shaded them.

Other historical Boab specimens grow around Timber Creek in the Northern Territory. The most famous of these is the Gregory Tree, which grows close to the banks of the Victoria River. This tree marks a stage of the North Australian Exploring Expedition led by Augustus Charles Gregory, which explored the Victoria River basin in 1855–56.

In 1855 the expedition ship, the schooner *Tom Tough*, went aground and was damaged near the mouth of the Victoria River. While one party rowed upstream to collect fresh water, the ship's surgeon, Mr Elsey, established a temporary camp near a natural spring. The men ferried their many livestock and supplies from the crippled vessel to the campsite.

Some months later, when the rains broke, Augustus Gregory and several other members of the party, including the versatile artist, storeman and factotum Thomas Baines, explored upriver and found an ideal camping site near a group of Gouty-stem Trees. In a small tributary not far from the camp they came across a stand of tall Melaleuca or paperbark trees which furnished timber suitable for repairing the ship, as well as long strips of bark which the men used as roofing material for their huts. They named the tributary Timber Creek.

With a detachment of men and thirty horses, Augustus Gregory explored further upstream and found a site suitable for a Depot camp, where he proposed to transfer stores and livestock in readiness for his overland journey to Brisbane. Baines was given the task of setting this up: no mean feat, given that the Depot's distance from the Principal camp near Timber Creek was about a hundred kilometres as the crow flies, further again from the *Tom Tough*, and they were not flying like crows but sailing and rowing up tortuous rivers and creeks.

Gregory then led an exploratory party inland as far as the edge of the Great Sandy Desert. On his return he found the ship's repairs still incomplete and the expedition's supplies severely reduced through the combined effects of seawater contamination, rats, termites, and the heat and humidity. Gregory, who planned soon to set off on his overland expedition via the Gulf of Carpentaria to Brisbane, gave instructions for the schooner, as soon as it could sail, to travel to Koepang in Timor and take on board further supplies, then rendezvous with the overlanders at the Albert River in Carpentaria. Thomas Baines, who had proved himself resourceful in countless ways, was left in command.

the famous | Chapter 5

The next few weeks passed in a frenzy of activity to make the ship seaworthy and transfer the bulk of the remaining supplies upriver to the Depot for Gregory's party to carry overland.

A few days after Gregory's departure, Baines and his men dismantled the Depot camp and rejoined the *Tom Tough*, which then set sail for Timor. Before leaving the Principal camp, Baines carved messages in two trees. According to Russell Braddon's account based on Baines' diaries, one read: OCTOBER 13TH 1855 — JULY 2ND 1856 LETTER IN OVEN. The second tree was carved with the words: LETTER IN FORGE. The letters gave details of the expedition's activities for the benefit of any future explorers and to establish a prior claim.

When the overland expedition led by Augustus Gregory reached the Albert River sooner than expected, on August 31st, the supply ship and its crew, who had been engaged in a number of melodramas of their own resulting in their having to abandon the *Tom Tough* and hire the *Messenger* in its place, had not arrived. Gregory's party still had ample supplies for the rest of their journey to Brisbane, and they decided to leave without waiting for their support vessel.

The Gregory tree is still boldly marked with the date, July 2nd 1856. However, there is no evidence of the earlier date, and the rest of the message has been partly obscured by more recent markings. Not unexpectedly, there is no sign of a forge or oven.

Although this tree can only be approached along several kilometres of a rough and very bumpy car track, it evidently draws enough visitors to be in danger of vandalism. Nowadays, this once picturesque and welcoming shade tree, as shown in old Timber Creek postcards, is surrounded by an ugly mesh fence, with barbed wire running along the top and foot. Photographs must

the famous | Chapter 5

July 2nd 1856

Letter in Oven　　　　　　　　　　　　The Gregory Tree, NT

either be marred by the fence eyesore, or obtained at too-close quarters by a photographer who is prepared to endure snags to person and/or clothing by rolling under the fence and over the barbed wire, as I did. (One can spare one's clothing by taking it off.) I wonder whether the site is not more spoiled by the presence of the fence than it would be by occasional tourists who insist on immortalising themselves alongside Gregory and his party.

It was on this expedition that Mueller, the botanist, identified the Australian Gouty-stem Tree as the second known member of the genus *Adansonia*, and named it *A. gregorii*, after Captain Gregory, the expedition's Commander.

Another notable but less venerable Boab near Timber Creek stands at the turn-off to Bullita. This is the 'Government Tree' with H. E. Le Hunte's name neatly carved in the side, and dated 1906. Le Hunte was an administrative aide to the Governor-General, conducting an official tour of the Victoria River District when he camped under that tree. He or one of his party commemorated his stay with the inscription.

About ten kilometres from Timber Creek back on the Kununurra road is a sizeable Boab tree, also carved with the date 1906, marking the grave of a young drover named John Lawle, who lies buried at its foot. The simple hand-engraved tin plaque nailed to the tree above the grave informs the visitor that Lawle was thirty-three years old when he died.

Fitzmaurice River Tree

An intriguing discovery made public as recently as 1997 was the mysterious inscription on a Boab tree on Bradshaw Station on the Fitzmaurice River in the Northern Territory. The tree is carved with the date 1814, which is several decades before the first known expedition by European explorers of the area. It also bears some wording, no longer decipherable, which appears to be a latinate name. There has been speculation that the date was carved by an otherwise unrecorded Portuguese visitor to the coast, perhaps a member of a reconnaissance team of seamen exploring the Fitzmaurice, but no corroborative evidence has yet been found.

Bernadette Masters of the University of Sydney has visited the tree and photographed it, taking tracings of the date and other markings she discovered on the trunk. Dr Masters, a mediaevalist, tells me that the so-called Portuguese writing is in fact Latin, and the other markings are neo-mediaeval Christian images. She has written a paper that discusses the origins of these markings.

Darrell Lewis of the Northern Territory Research Unit tells me he has recorded more than a hundred trees in the Victoria River District with

the famous | Chapter 5

historic markings, including names of explorers and drawings and designs by both Aboriginal people and Europeans.

We return to the Kimberley, to Camden Harbour, site of an ill-starred attempt at early settlement by the Camden Harbour Pastoral Association. Inspired by reports of 'luxuriant vegetation', 'plentiful animals, birds and fish' and especially 'millions of acres of good pastoral country', three groups of would-be settlers including women and children set off from Melbourne in 1864 aboard three vessels with their stores, furniture, horses and 4,500 merino sheep. They arrived at Camden Harbour in December, the hottest, driest time of the year. They found rocks and dead grass instead of the seasonal 'splendid pasture and abundant water' seen by members of a gold-seeking expedition which had visited the Harbour earlier in the year, just following the wet.

Camden Harbour

The small area of pasture around the one freshwater spring near the shore was insufficient for the stock, and the sheep died in flocks. The first human fatality was Captain Edwards, who had been a passenger in the *Calliance* which struck a reef and broke up. Edwards sailed to Timor in the ship's cutter to charter a replacement, but the schooner he was bringing back capsized and Edwards drowned. There would be others. The bodies of six of them were buried at Sheep Island, a tiny, rocky island just out of Kuri Bay.

The intending settlers, most of whom were moneyed and unused to manual labour, were quickly demoralised. They made little attempt to establish permanent settlement, and almost none accepted allocations of land. They started to leave as soon as ships called in, selling off their goods for almost nothing to those who remained as Government officials or because they could not afford to pay their passage out.

R. J. Sholl, the Magistrate who had been sent up to administer the settlement, presided instead over the departures. He also officiated at burials. On May 18th 1865, Sholl's son Treverton recorded the death of 'poor Jimba, our native boy', who joined two settlers at Sheep Island, where the Magistrate read the burial service for him.

On June 4th, Jimba was followed by Mrs Mary Jane Pascoe, aged thirty, who died of 'remittant fever' after delivering a baby. Mrs Pascoe was laid to rest at the foot of a sturdy Boab tree which stands a short climb up from the little shell-grit beach. Her headstone is the only one still standing, the grave itself marked out by large stones. Other graves are now covered with a tangle of vegetation. The marker stones are still there, but disarranged, and the other headstones, some of which were wooden and others said to have been made of metal, were long ago eaten by termites or stolen by Macassan fishermen.

The Boab tree that witnessed all these burials has suffered many cuts and markings, some evidently quite old. I. M. Crawford, writing in 1968, says that Mary Pascoe's name was carved on that tree at the time of her burial, and was still 'perfectly legible' when he visited. Thirty years later most of the markings, including Mary's name, had grown over and were hard or impossible to make out in full.

The tree also bears a small metal plaque, inscribed: IN MEMORY OF PC WALTER GEE DIED SEPTEMBER 1865 SPEARED BY NATIVES WHILE ON DUTY WITH SCHOLL [sic] EXPEDITION.

Constable Gee was a member of a party of six led by Magistrate Sholl who set off in a pinnace to find and retrieve one of the other Government boats which had been stolen by Aborigines resentful of the settlers' intrusion. When the party went ashore to rest, they were attacked by a large band of the local inhabitants armed with fighting sticks and spears. Young

opposite: Limestone Gorge, Gregory National Park, NT

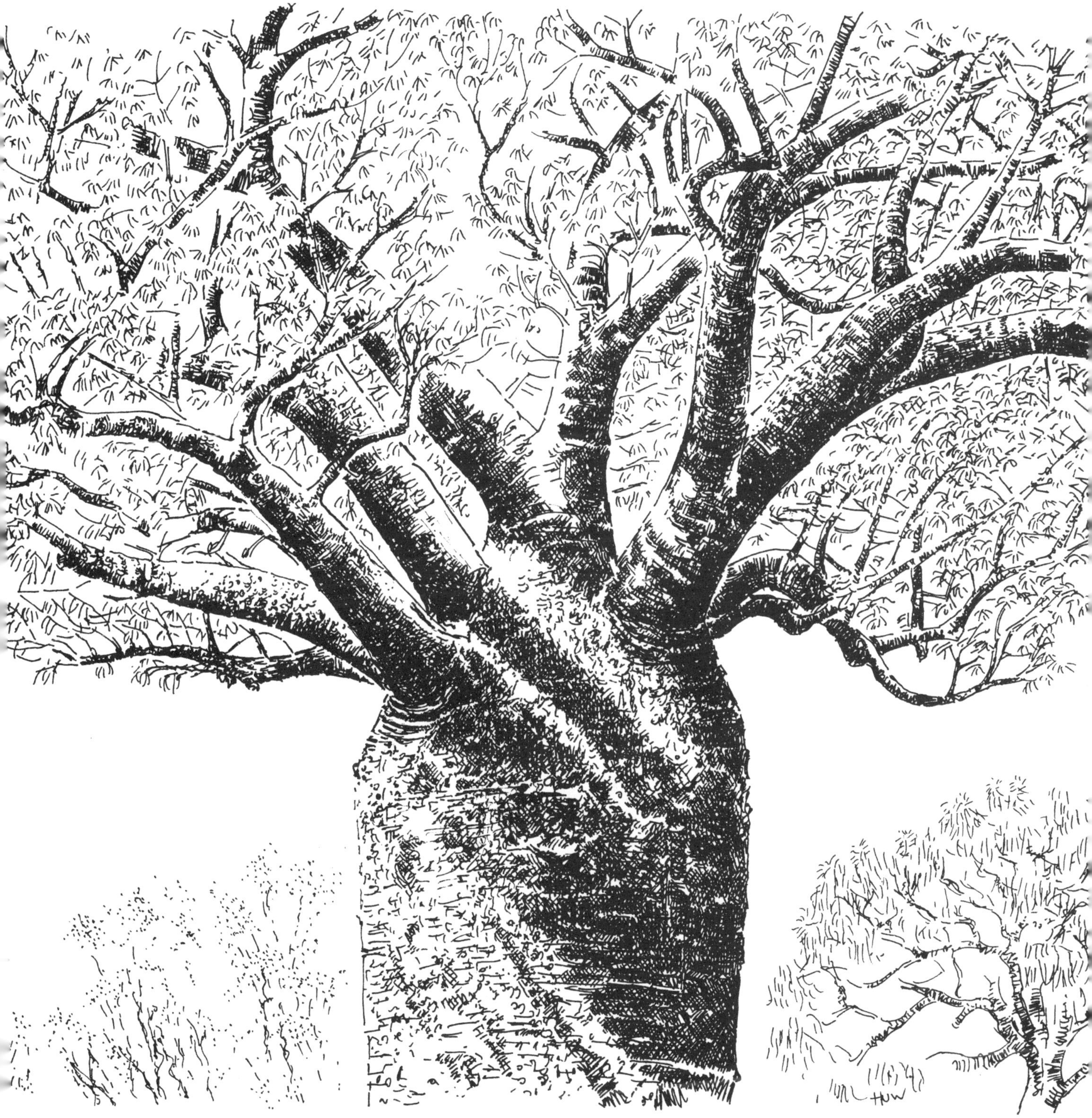

the famous | Chapter 5

Treverton Sholl and Constable Gee both suffered spear wounds, Sholl to the arm and Gee to the shoulder.

The whites retaliated by opening fire, killing and wounding an unrecorded number of their attackers. They reached their boat and rowed away, struggling against the tide. When they stopped to rest and wait for the right time to continue, their anchor caught fast and the tide tugging at the boat pulled the bow underwater. The men were all thrown out into the racing sea. One of their number, E. Quinlan, drowned, but the others managed eventually to struggle ashore. T. Tomkinson, who became separated from the others, made his way back to Camden Harbour where he reported that everyone else but Gee had been lost. A party was sent out to search for Gee, but meanwhile the survivors managed to make their way tortuously back to camp. It took them four days to cover the forty kilometres.

Treverton Sholl and the others recovered but Walter Gee died on August 17th, leaving a widow with four children; a fifth was born two months later. It seems that the plaque on the Boab tree is inaccurate by one month. It was probably put up relatively recently, Gee's grave having long since crumbled into the bush.

Russell Hanigan of Paspaley Pearls first told me about the graveyard at Sheep Island, when he heard that I was writing about Boab trees. It wasn't for another year that I approached John Woodman about getting out there. After an anxious wait for several weeks until a seat could be found for me on the weekly flight to Kuri Bay, I flew in one brilliant blue and white morning, landing in the sea-plane on the smooth water of the harbour. When everyone was safely ashore and getting ready for work on the pearl farm, Harry Hooper, the skipper of the boat that met us from the plane, took me out to Sheep Island. 'I have to warn you,' Harry told me before we left, 'the last people who went over to the island were almost attacked by a three-metre crocodile. Just thought you ought to know.'

'This could be more exciting than I expected,' I said.

We motored off across the calm sea, and in no time we were putting ashore on the little beach at Sheep Island, mangroves on one side, rocks above. There was no sign of the crocodile, but Harry armed himself with a stick just in case. I was more willing to put my trust in Providence than in the stick. Harry stayed to watch the boat and let out the anchor chain as the tide fell while I explored the tiny, rocky island and photographed its Boab trees and Mary Pascoe's grave.

Perhaps I took a little longer in returning to the boat than I should have done, for hardly had we pushed off from the beach than the hull grated gently onto a submerged rock. The propeller of the outboard motor, which Harry had to raise a little to prevent it striking the bottom, was not powerful enough to push us off the rock on which we were pivoting, and the falling tide was about to make matters worse. Crocodiles or not, Harry wasn't going to keep us swinging there until the tide changed. Asking me to keep an eye out for unfriendly reptiles, he was over the side, had shoved the boat free and was back on board again in the blink of a crocodile's eyelid.

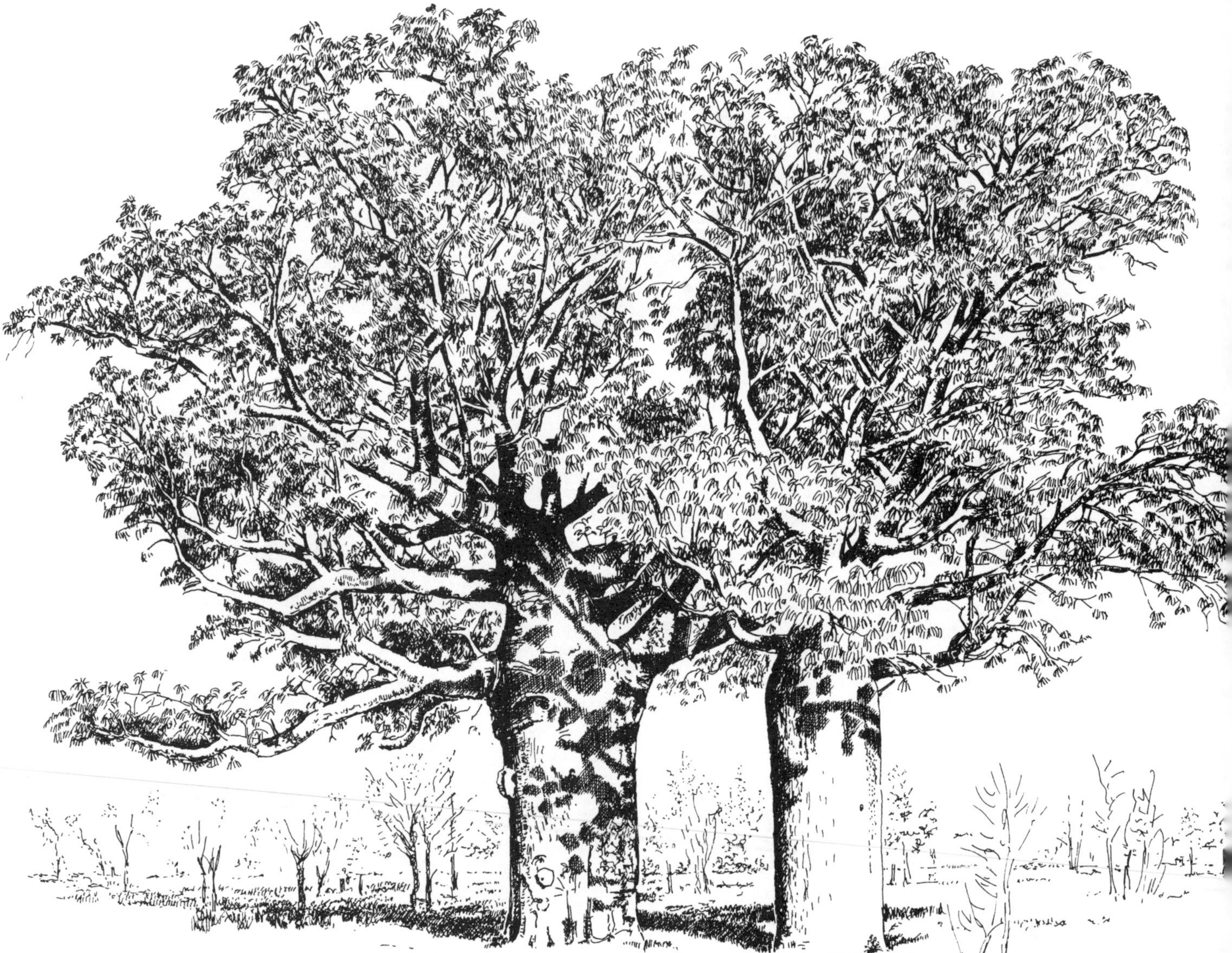
HUW

home life | Chapter 6

This great, bulky, long-lived tree, whose bark is inclined to become folded and pocked with age, creates a climate in its shade noticeably cooler and more humid than that of the surrounding scrub. These conditions provide a habitat for many species of animals and birds. The sturdy branches offer safe supports for nests which become well-concealed from predators during the season when the tree is in leaf.

A careful inspection of any big tree is likely to reveal the nests of several bird species. Most obvious is the large and untidy assemblage of wooden twigs put together by the crow and often later colonised by the Fork-tailed Kite — that impressive-looking raptor with the reputation, celebrated in creation stories, of being a poor hunter because it lives on insects and carrion and does not kill large game of its own. In contrast to this is the neat, smooth, cup-shaped mud-nest of the Magpie-lark, whose terracotta nursery must surely have inspired human beings to build houses from rammed earth.

Pairs of Grey-crowned Babblers work together to put up their roughly globular nests of sticks and grass. From my perch in the fork of one massive tree I have watched what looked like a *ménage à trois* attending to the same nest, but the odd male out was soon sent on his way unthanked by his rival.

Some birds, including kestrels, take advantage of pockets or hollows high up in the tree, which they line with grass and twigs and use as nests for their eggs. The nests' whereabouts are betrayed by deposits of bird lime coating the tree underneath. One hot November I stopped at a spreading Boab near the roadside, and noticed a hawk-like bird perched on a root, watching me. I got out my camera, and slowly walked towards the bird, which I later identified as a Nankeen Kestrel. To my surprise, the bird allowed me to approach quite closely. I soon realised it was a young bird that had probably fallen from its nest. It was fully fledged, but not yet able to fly. When I came

opposite: Mother and daughter, Ivanhoe Crossing, East Kimberley, WA

home life | Chapter 6

too close, it hopped and fluttered away to a perch at a more comfortable distance.

Later, I returned and sat with the kestrel, which soon got used to my presence. I lay down in front of its low perch to bring myself to the same level, and carefully put out my hand. The kestrel allowed me to touch its wing, and even, miraculously, stepped onto my finger.

Over the next few weeks I returned several times to visit the young kestrel, and was always surprised to find it still hopping around the foot of the same tree. Sometimes I found it sheltering in a recess formed by the roots. Once or twice, when I was sitting quietly nearby, a parent bird flew into the tree above. Then the young one, its head turned sideways so that it could look upwards, scurried towards the tree trunk, excitedly calling out. I didn't see the mother bird feed its offspring but, once, I

PAGE 80

above: The young kestrel
opposite: The kestrel tree in the dry season, showing a kite's nest in the upper branches, near the Broome–Derby road, not far from Logue River

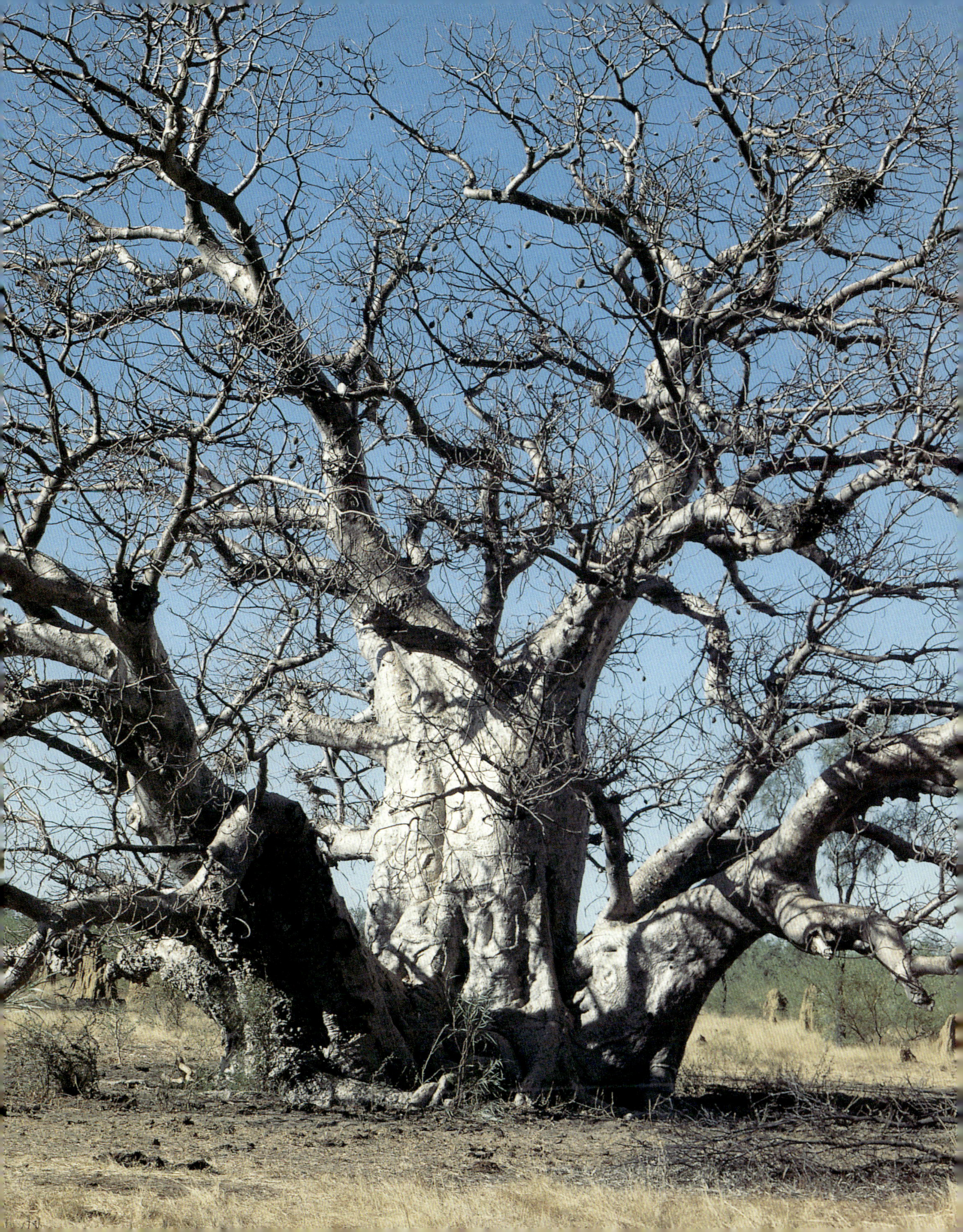

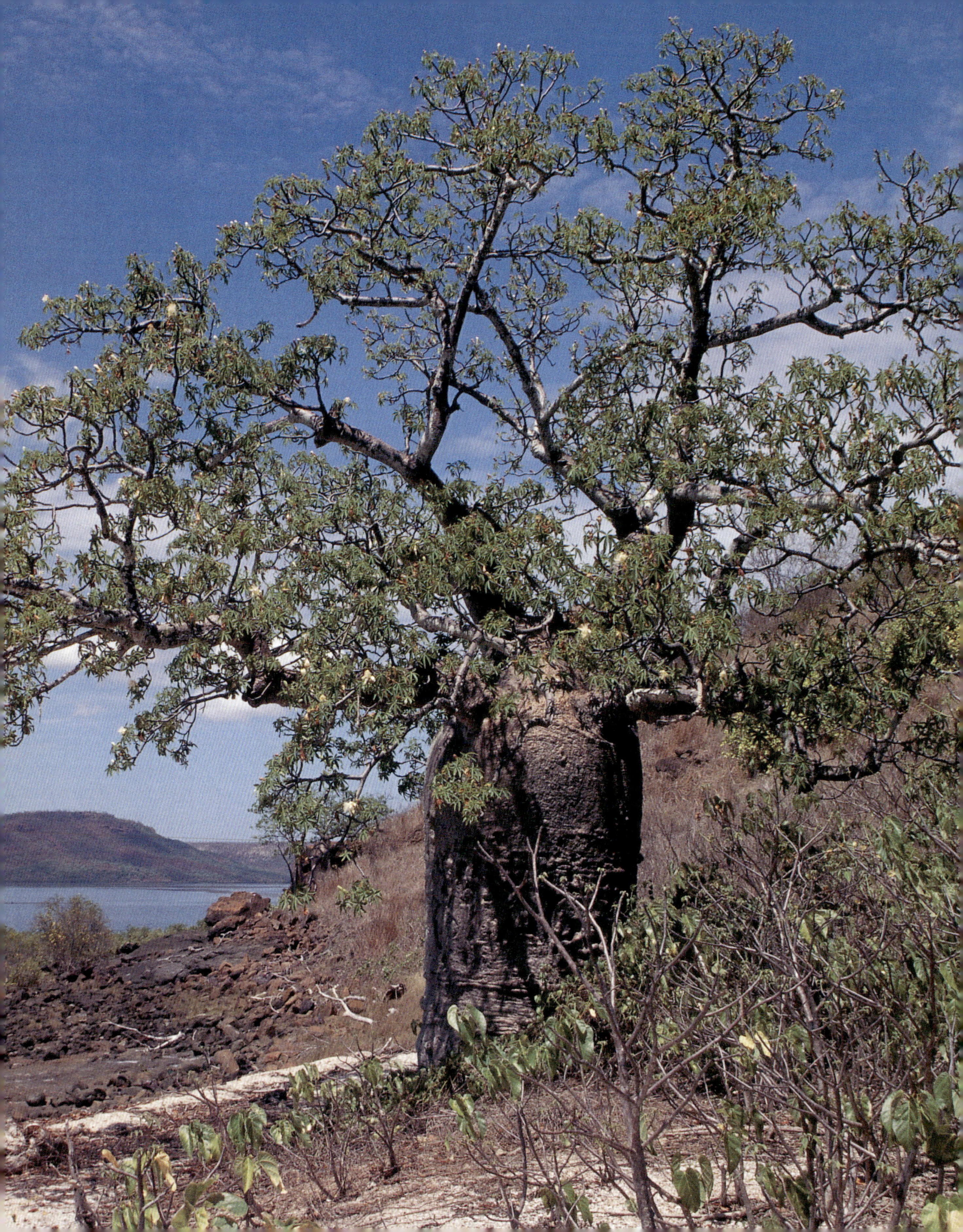

home life | Chapter 6

saw the young bird, on its own, catch and demolish a small lizard.

After an absence of a couple of weeks, I returned to the tree but could find no sign of the kestrel, apart from deposits of bird droppings on the tree-roots where it liked to sit. I walked away and paused some distance from the tree. Then I heard the unmistakable repeated call of the young kestrel to its mother. I was unable to find its new hiding place, and I left, hoping that this change of activity marked a growing independence.

It was a month before I returned to that tree, in late January, after a spell of unseasonably dry weather. I climbed to the first fork in the squat trunk and looked over. On the ground on the other side lay the desiccated remains of a bird of prey. Though its body had been partly eaten by ants, there were enough feathers left, particularly on its tail, for me to identify it as a kestrel. Perhaps, after all, the young bird had never learnt to fly.

The Logue River grove trees provide breeding sites for many different kinds of birds. I have seen Fork-tailed Kites nesting there, their platform of sticks providing a strong support for the grassy nests of a colony of Zebra Finches breeding at the same time underneath. Whether the sitting kite and her offspring were disturbed or entertained by the comings and goings of their noisy neighbours in the lower apartment I am unable to say.

In a Boab tree nearby I caught a glimpse of a grey bird; at first I thought it was a pigeon, but it proved to be too big. With the help of binoculars I identified it as a White-faced Heron, sitting on the scrappiest little nest which looked as if it would hardly have room to support a growing chick. Yet on my next visit several weeks later, I found the mother heron in the same place alongside a smaller edition of herself. Both birds sat motionless with their long necks stretched and their beaks pointed to the sky, so that they were barely distinguishable from the grey branches around them.

breeding sites

opposite: Boab tree on Sheep Island near Kuri Bay. Several members of the ill-fated Camden Harbour expedition are buried in the shade of this tree.

home life : Chapter 6

Not all birds that visit Boab trees build nests in them. As we have already seen, honey-eaters feed on the early morning nectar of the flowers, and may thereby assist in pollination. Others take advantage of the shade offered by the Boab's foliage in the heat of the day or forage amongst the branches for insects and lizards. Approach a large and shady Boab on a hot day, and you are likely to startle out of its crown a flurry of white cockatoos, a pair of honey-eaters, a sleepy and indignant owl.

It pays to approach a large Boab cautiously, scanning its crown with binoculars to spot its inhabitants before you disturb them. The Grandmother tree near Logue River has one conspicuous window which twice in one day rewarded such caution. The first time, from a distance, I could see the head of a bird which I took to be a frogmouth. When I reached the tree the head was gone, but after a few minutes of hiding behind the trunk I peered around it and looked up into the startled eyes of an Owlet-Nightjar. It took off from its hollow and landed higher up the trunk before departing for a quieter perch. Later the same day I came back and inspected the tree through binoculars, hoping the bird had returned. Sure enough, there at the window appeared a head, but a different one. I skirted the tree and again emerged under the hollow, peering upwards. This time I found myself looking into the face of a goanna, bending its long neck the better to watch me with intensely disapproving yellow eyes.

Buzzard Tree

One hot season I visited a particular Boab almost every weekend over a couple of months. I'd have a midday snack with a billy of tea and an afternoon snooze under its branches. Directly above my head was the nest of a pair of Black-breasted Buzzards. I noticed the parent birds flying overhead in the vicinity of the tree, but it wasn't until one of them passed close by that any sounds issued from the nest, betraying its occupant.

home life | Chapter 6

I read somewhere that the Black-breasted Buzzard incubates two eggs until they hatch, but rears only a single chick. The macabre explanation for the missing chick is that the stronger one devours its sibling. I never saw the hatchlings, but only one chick grew to maturity in this nest.

Over the weeks that I watched, I was privileged several times to see the chick being fed by its parent. She, if indeed it was the mother, used to fly in around the middle of the day, circling first and calling to the chick, who called back with audible excitement. Then, with a swish of wings, she would plunge down through the branches, carrying a small animal in her claws, and land on the nest. I would hear cluckings of pleasure from the chick as the prey was passed over, and then the mother would be off again to continue her ceaseless hunt.

In the debris under the nest, I picked up the bony remains of several lizards and the skull of a Tawny Frogmouth. A couple of times my dogs, which have been trained to hunt, caught and killed small goannas in the neighbourhood of the tree, not big or fat enough to be worth cooking to eat. I would leave the goannas draped on a nearby antbed, an offering to the buzzard. Each time I came back, the goanna had disappeared, but whether it had been picked up by the buzzard and fed to her offspring, or taken by another bird or animal, I cannot say.

After a few weeks the young bird was big enough to look over the side of its nest and contemplate the supine form underneath, holding its head on one side to eye me dubiously. I watched the comings and goings around the nest until the young bird had learnt to fly. After that I usually found it perched on the dead branch of a eucalypt that stood near the Boab. Sometimes I found a parent bird sitting there beside it. The adult flew off as I approached but the young one stayed put, and I liked to think it had become

home life | Chapter 6

so used to my presence over the weeks of its infancy that it did not consider me a threat. It also crossed my mind that a bird with less than normal fear of people might put itself in danger.

One Sunday I made my way to the Buzzard Tree and found the remains nearby of someone else's recent fire. For the first time, the young bird was neither in its nest nor on its perch. I approached the ashes. There, beside the fireplace, lay plucked feathers, pieces of a bird: my worst fears come to pass. I bent to examine the remains. And realised, with callous relief, that I was looking at a pair of duck wings.

The following year I hoped to watch the next generation of Black-breasted Buzzards growing up, but whenever I visited the Boab tree a Fork-tailed Kite flew out of its branches. There was no evidence of further nest-building, and no sign of life in the nest. One day in early March, I stopped at the tree for a rest and fell asleep in its deep shade. When I woke up, I noticed a small bundle of yellowish fluff close to my feet. This turned out to be the limp body of a downy young chick, fallen from the nest. Its wings were no more than unformed flaps, and only the curved dark beak, absurdly fierce for such a tiny owner, identified the body as that of a baby raptor.

This same tree, stout and mature but not yet pocked and senescent, must be a venerable age already. Nearby my companion, Jimmy Pike, found one day a smooth stone tool that an unknown woman of the region, seated in the shade, had once used for grinding seeds. The stone fits comfortably in the hand, and is well worn.

The multiple nooks that an old tree acquires in its trunk give shelter to insects and other little arthropods. Families of crickets huddle in the cool shade of one hollow, while another is loud with the song of a cloud of mosquitoes. Colonies of ants go about their business up and down the trunk and

opposite: Ivanhoe, East Kimberley, WA

home life | Chapter 6

amongst the lower branches, or make nests in the debris that builds up in crannies formed by the exposed upper surface of the roots. A fat-bodied orb-weaving spider spins her web in the crotch of a branch. Clusters of bagmoth larvae take advantage of safe crannies, where they attach their cases and in their own good time transform themselves into moths. A species of narrow-bodied black beetle with brown antennae seems to be at home on Boab trunks; more rarely, a solitary jewel beetle gleams there.

In the sand at the foot of a young Boab my dog once dug up the enormous white, fat curl-grub larva of a scarab beetle. I moved the grub to a similar spot under another tree, loosened the packed sand, and watched it dig its way down into the ground, using its head and legs as excavation tools.

home life | Chapter 6

Native bees, those benign, blunt, stingless insects that look like little flies and are attracted to sweaty skin, sometimes build their nests inside suitable cavities. They reveal their presence by the sound of their collective humming. These bees fashion fine dark waxy tubes, pliable to the touch, through which they move between their nests and the world outside.

A burly tree near Logue River bridge must have been a favoured stopping place for travellers in the 1920s, a number of whom, amongst them a Mr and Mrs Bagg, have left names and dates carved at various heights in its bark. One day, when I was exploring with my pen torch one of the many little clefts and holes in this tree, a gecko I had unwittingly disturbed rushed out suddenly, causing me to drop my torch. It ran higher up the tree and tried vainly to conceal itself in a crack in the bark. When I came back a couple of hours later and again probed the hole, the same gecko ran out, and tried to hide in another inadequate crack. Perhaps deciding that its usual hideout was altogether too dangerous a place, it didn't return that afternoon, but tried its luck hunting insects by daylight instead.

Another niche in the same tree held a large and very sluggish moth which, because of its failure to react to my touch, I took at first to be dead. However, when I tried to pick it up it tetchily shifted position, so I left it alone. I supposed that it too was sleeping away the day in preparation for an active and perhaps exciting night, when it could very well find itself being pursued, if not eaten, by the gecko from next door.

bark damage

While the trunk of a relatively young Boab appears smooth, that of a very old one displays flaky patches, often marked out around the perimeter as if by a knife, which can easily be prised away. Beneath the flaked surface the woody substance looks diseased. It is dark, soft and loose, and can be scraped out with a pocket knife. I have found beetles and centipedes con-

home life | Chapter 6

cealed within this debris, but its main inhabitant, offspring of the apparent culprit responsible for the damage, is a tiny, thread-like larva which pupates within a fragile brown case. When the contents of a damaged patch are removed, they leave a small cavity. Such is perhaps the origin of many of the little hollows that so characterise the trunk of an old Boab.

Over time, the hollows and cavities collect blown dust and debris, a rich soil in which air- or bird-borne seeds may germinate when conditions are moist, forming ephemeral miniature gardens. Once the season changes and the soil dries out, the seedlings die.

One Christmas Day, early in the wet season, when I was climbing an ancient Boab growing near a creek to inspect its deep, tank-like hollow, I encountered a green tree frog sleeping in a niche about three metres above the ground. Tree frogs are creatures of habit who like to

tree frogs

top: Old tree with hollows
bottom: The tool found by Jimmy Pike near the Buzzard Tree

home life | Chapter 6

PAGE 88

above: Hardman Creek, West Kimberley, WA
inset: Startled frog

home life | Chapter 6

return to the same sleeping quarters each morning, after their night's hunting activities. I know this from my observations of tree frogs who have taken up residence in my house. One used to favour the dome of my upturned wok on a cupboard shelf, where every morning she would be found sleeping, hands folded like a little buddha, but from where she always vanished to conduct her hunting forays around the kitchen at night. Others favour the space between the bathroom wall and the sliding door. Most prefer to stay in the wet interior of the toilet cistern, or hidden under the lip of the toilet bowl — a position which has its perils when the toilet is flushed. At the time of writing, one has been living for the past couple of weeks under my hat on the kitchen shelf.

It seems probable, therefore, that the frog I met in the Boab spent most of its wet season life in the tree, emerging from the cavity at dark to hunt its insect prey amongst the branches, and returning home each morning at first light. There is, during the wet, enough water in the Boab's small hollows to meet the frog's needs, and only when, following heavy rain, it hears the urgent carolling of other frogs must it leave the tree and answer the summons to amplexus in the brimming creek below.

A month after first meeting the Boab tree frog, I went back to the same place, and was delighted to find the frog still there in its niche. It must have been sleeping out on the threshold because, as my head drew level with the hollow, the frog hastily pulled back inside. A week or so later still, I visited the frog again and, leaning perilously out from my perch, took its photograph. The flash must have penetrated the inner depths of the hollow, because a short time later I was startled to see two frogs, side by side. I photographed the couple, and within minutes they had been joined by a third.

Exactly a year later I returned to this tree, but found no tree frog in

home life | Chapter 6

residence. However, from the deep hollow in the trunk issued the distinctive smell of guano. I peered down through a hole in the top of the trunk between the main branches, which admitted just enough light to reveal bats, disturbed by my climbing, flitting silently back and forth across the space inside.

On station country, home of many Boabs, cattle wander up to stand and ruminate in the dense shade of a leafy tree in the heat of the afternoon. During the late dry season, when other food is scarce, they browse on fallen nuts. When a Boab tree at last falls down, cattle will eat the fibrous interior of the trunk which, though not appetising to look at, and probably not much better to taste, even for a cow, contains moisture and some nutrients.

Once I explored a massive old Boab growing at the edge of a claypan near the Gibb River Road. There were the usual arthropod residents and a fair-sized goanna that came scuttling out of the undergrowth and fled. I made my way around the tree's enormous girth, and suddenly found myself looking down on a skeleton. A dog — perhaps a dingo — had chosen the deep shade of this tree as a place to die. The skeleton was complete. Patches of skin, dry and papery, still clung to the bones, a few fawn hairs attached.

Later, I took Jimmy Pike to see this tree and its companion skeleton, and he told me that he had heard of a hollow tree somewhere nearby where the bodies of murder victims were said to have been stowed. By tacit agreement we found ourselves examining all the likely-looking Boab trees for human remains, but our macabre search went unrewarded.

It is not only animals and birds that benefit from the microclimate created by a closely growing grove of Boabs, or even by a single large tree. Particular associations of plants flourish in their immediate neighbourhood. A mistletoe, *Dendrophthoe acacioides*, more usually hosted by acacia or grevillea species, is also sometimes found growing on Boab trees around Derby.

home life : Chapter 6

In the dry season, when the Boab loses its leaves, the surrounding grasses and shrubs all die off, and the country presents a uniformly dry, burnt and dead appearance to the passer-by. Following good rain, the scene is quickly transformed. Not only is the Boab in leaf, but the seeds of other plants that have lain dormant now burst into life all around. Grass springs up first, green and lush, followed by the annual shrubs. The Conkerberry bush, *Carissa lanceolata,* favours the Boab's shade, as does *Abrus precatorius,* the Crab's Eye Bean, a liane with attractive but highly toxic shiny scarlet and black seeds. As these plants come into flower, a variety of butterflies, dragonflies and damselflies lend a touch of fairyland to the ephemeral luxuriance.

IS THERE SUCH A THING as vegetative awareness? Do trees experience anything of the world around them? Are they perhaps diffusely conscious? There are those who believe that plants can think and feel, and those who deny that any living creatures other than human beings are aware at all. The truth may be, as truth so often is, somewhere in between.

It is unlikely that plants can think. For that they would require a brain and nervous system. However, it is also true that plants respond to certain stimuli. All plants are sensitive to sunlight and darkness, while insectivorous and trigger plants react even to an insect's delicate touch. There is a sense in which plants are more aware than, say, water or a rock.

It can be interesting to speculate on what a long-lived Boab tree may have witnessed in the course of its long life, whether the information has registered somewhere in its massive form or not. A tree aged a mere few hundred years would have grown to maturity when the Kimberley was Paradise. It would have provided shade, food and very likely water for generation after generation of the local people. It would have presided over their

home life : Chapter 6

economic and domestic activities. It would have sheltered women as they gave birth and raised their young, as they rested from hunting, as they prepared food for their families; men as they cooked game and manufactured tools. It would have witnessed ceremonies, and listened to countless songs.

Its tough bark would have been singed by many a bush fire, shed layers and recovered. It would be both the matriarch and the patriarch of scores of generations of descendants. Its branches would have supported the nests of countless birds, season after season. Billions and more insects would have wandered over the surface of its trunk and branches, going about their inscrutable business.

The same tree would have witnessed the arrival in its country of the first Europeans. It would have given shade to weary explorers, and later to the first settlers and their stock. It would have noticed great changes that followed in the local people's lives; watched them adopt many of the ways of the Europeans. It may have witnessed bloodshed, heard rumours of massacre. In its advancing years, it would have listened to the overhead noise of the engines of the first aircraft to cross Australian skies. It would have felt the vibrations of war.

And even today, such a tree could not be described as old. With perhaps another millennium of life ahead of it, it will see events we cannot yet imagine. Who knows, perhaps that very tree will be witness to the passing of the human race. By the time it finally falls and dies, it may barely remember that we ever existed.

the eight baobabs of the world

THE AUSTRALIAN BOAB
Adansonia gregorii

Kalumburu
Careening Bay
Camden Harbour
Kuri Bay
Sheep Island
Wyndham
Fitzmaurice River
Bradshaw Station
Kununurra
Timber Creek
Bullida
Karunji Station
Gibb River Road
Pt Torment
Derby
Meda Station
Fitzroy River
Ord River
Victoria River
Logue River
Broome
Mt Anderson Station
Looma Community
Fitzroy Crossing
Halls Creek
Highway One
WA / NT

THE AFRICAN BAOBAB
Adansonia digitata

possibly introduced into West Africa

THE SIX BAOBAB SPECIES OF MADAGASCAR

Adansonia perrieri
Adansonia suarezensis
Adansonia madagascariensis

Adansonia grandidieri
Adansonia za
Adansonia fony

bibliography

Armstrong, P., 'Baobabs – Remnant of Gondwanaland?' in *New Scientist*, 73, pp. 212–13, 1977.
—'The Boab Tree' in *Australian Plants*, 9: pp. 226–9, 1977.
—'The disjunct distribution of the genus Adansonia' in *National Geographic Journal of India*, Vol. 29, 142–63, 1983.
Bash, Barbara, *The Tree of Life*, Sierra Club Books, Little Brown & Co., 1989.
Basedow, Herbert, *Narrative of an Expedition in North-Western Australia*, W. K. Thomas & Co., 1918.
Baum, David, 'The Comparative Pollination and Floral Biology of Baobabs (*Adansonia*-Bombacaceae)', *Ann. Missouri Bot. Gard.*, 82, 1955, pp. 322–48.
—'A Systematic Revision of *Adansonia* (Bombacaceae)', *ibid.*, pp. 440–70, 1995.
Bingham, M. G., 'Did the Baobabs Originate in Madagascar?' in *Ingens Bulletin* 10, April 1994.
Braddon, Russell, *Thomas Baines and the North Australian Expedition*, Collins, Sydney in association with the Royal Geographical Society, 1986.
Coates, Yvonne & Kevin, *Lonely Graves of Western Australia & Burials at Sea*, Hesperian Press, 1986.
Crawford, I. M., *The Art of the Wandjina: Aboriginal Cave Paintings in the Kimberley WA*, Oxford University Press, Melbourne, 1968.
—'Traditional Aboriginal Plant Resources in the Kalumburu Area' in *Aspects in Ethnoeconomics*, WA Museum, Perth, 1982.
Flora of Australia Vol. 22: 'Rhizophorales to Celastrales', Bureau of Flora & Fauna, Australian Government Publishing Service, Canberra, 1984.
Hiddins, Les, *Survive to Live* An analysis of survival and its relationship in Northern Australia, Commonwealth Govt Printer, Canberra, 1981.
Hordern, Marsden, *Mariners Be Warned!*, Melbourne University Press, 1989.
—*King of the Australian Coast*, The Miegunyah Press, MUP, 1997.
Jalakbiya, Molly, 'Wajarri: The Boab Nut' in *Thangani Bunuba*, KLRC, 1998.
Kenneally K., Edinger D.C., & Willing T., *Broome and Beyond*, Department of Conservation and Land Management, WA, 1996.
Mueller F., 'Botanical Report on the North Australian Expedition, under the command of A.C. Gregory, Esq.', *Proc. Linn. Soc. Lond. (Bot)*, Vol. 2, p. 140, 1858.
Nangan, Joe, & Edwards, Hugh, *Joe Nangan's Dreaming*, Thomas Nelson (Australia) Ltd, 1976.
Peasley, J., 'From the de Grey to the Overland Telegraph Line (1879)' in *Early Days*, Journal of the Royal WA Historical Society (Inc.), Vol. 8, Part 4, Feb. 1980.
Richards, Christopher, *There Were Three Ships*, University of Western Australia Press, 1990.
Sculthorpe, Gaye, 'Designs on Carved Boab Nuts', in *COMA Bulletin*, No. 23, pp. 37–47, 1990.
Swart, E. R, 'Age of the Baobab Tree' in *Nature*, May 15th, 1963.,
Wickens, G. E. 'The Baobab: Africa's Upside-down Tree' in *Kew Bulletin*, Vol. 37, No. 2, 1982.
Willis, J. H., 'A bibliography of the Australian baobab' in *Muelleria*, 1, pp. 61–3, 1955.
Withnell, Taylor, Nancy E, *Yeera-Muk-A-Doo*, Fremantle Arts Centre Press, 1980.

index

Aboriginal people 37–51, 58–9, 65, 67, 72, 74
Abrus precatorius 91
Adanson, Michel 16
Adansonia spp. 12–13
    digitata 10, 14, 16, 20, 35
    gibbosa 17, 19
    gregorii 10. 14, 16, 19, 71
    madagascariensis 14, 19, 27
Aepyornis 15
Africa 10, 11, 14, 50
'Africa's Upside-Down Tree' 16
Akerman, Kim 58, 60
Albert River 69, 70
Alpino, Prospero 16
animal life 21, 79–90
Arabian peninsula 10
Armstrong, Patrick 11
arthropods 84–7
Art of the Wandjina, The 67
Augusta 15
Australian Museum 67

Bagg, Mr and Mrs 86
Baines, Thomas 43, 69, 70
baler shell 48
Bandignan 60
Barni 21
Barunga, Gordon 41
Basedow, Herbert 43, 58–60, 66, 67
bats 21, 26, 90
Baum, David 17, 25, 26, 28
Beagle, HMS 66
Berkeley Plain 49
bii 46, 48
Bingham, M. G. 14
bird life 79–84
Black-breasted Buzzards 82–4
Boab Festival 53
Boab Hotel 58
Bottle Tree, see *Brachychiton rupestris*
Brachychiton rupestris 40
Braddon, Russell 70

Bradshaw Station 72
Brisbane 69, 70
Broome 53–5
Brown, Stumpy 60
bu hibab 16
bu hobab 16
Bullita 72
Bunuba 48
Burrwan, Manuela 44
Buzzard Tree 82–4

Camden Harbour Expedition 73–7
Cairo 16
Calliance 73
Capparis 16, 63, 65
Careening Bay 63
Carissa lanceolata 91
Carpentaria, Gulf of 69
carved
    nuts 49, 50
    trees 67–73
Central America 11
Cervantes 15
Clarke, Max 55
Coco de Mer 15
Colac Roadhouse 53
Conkerberry Bush, see *Carissa lanceolata*
continental drift 10
Corkwood see *Gyrocarpus americanus*
Crab Creek 54
Crab's Eye Bean, see *Abrus precatorius*
Crawford, I. M. 67, 74
crocodile 77
crosses, ceremonial 48
Cunningham, Allan 64, 65

Daly River 51
Darwin, Charles 66
Darwin, NT 55
dehiscence 28
Dendrophthoe acacioides 90
Depot camp 69, 70
Derby 53–8, 60, 61
Devonian reef 15

dispersal 11, 14, 16, 29–30, 53–5
Done, Chris 30
Edwards, Captain 73
Elephant Bird, see *Aepyornis*
Elsey, Mr 68
Emmanuel Yard 67
eucalyptus 43
evolution 11, 14, 16
export 55

fibre 46–8
fire damage 32, 67
Fitzmaurice River 72
Fitzroy Crossing 32, 55–7, 60
Fitzroy River 66
flowers 23–7
flotation hypothesis 11
foliage 23, 31, 43, 48
food, Boab as 30, 41–4
Fork-tailed Kite 79, 81, 84
Forrest, Alexander 66
frogs 87–90
fruit 27–30, 41–3, 46, 50

Gantheaume Point 54
Gee, Walter 74–6
Gibb River Road 45, 54, 90
gibbosa 17, 19
Gondwanaland 10, 11
Gouty-stemmed Tree 63, 64, 69
Government Tree 72
Grandmother Tree 20, 82
Great Sandy Desert 69
Gregory, Augustus Charles 17, 19, 68–70
Gregory Tree 68, 70–1
Grey, George 63
Grey-crowned Babblers 79
Gulf of Carpentaria 69
Guniin 46
Gwini 46
Gyrocarpus americanus 11, 23

Half-way Tree 56–7
Hanigan, Russell 76
Hann River 68
hawkmoths 25–7

index

Helicopter Tree see *Gyrocarpus americanus*
Hicks, Arthur 66
Hill, Fenton 66
hollows 84–8
Hooper, Harry 76–7
Howard, Dennis and Margaret 45

Imintji 45
India 10
Indian Ocean 11, 14, 15
Indonesian seeds 15
invertebrates 21

Jimba 74
jumulu 46
Jussieu, Bernard de 16

Kalumburu 45, 48
Karunjie Station 68
Katherine 55
Kenya 29
Kerguelen Islands 15
kestrel, see Nankeen Kestrel
Kimberley 10, 15, 40, 50, 54, 56, 58, 63, 66, 68, 73
King, Captain Phillip Parker 17, 63–5
King Penguin 15
King Sound 53, 66
Knox, Gwen 56
Koepang 69
Kununurra 55
kuruwan 37
Kuri Bay 73, 76

larrkarti 37, 50
Lawle, John 72
leaves, see foliage
Le Hunte, H. E. 72
Lewis, Darrel 72
Linnaeus 16
Livingstone, David 20
Logue River 20, 55, 82
longevity 9, 19–20
Looma 39, 50
Love Tree 53
Lunganan, Daisy 39

Macassans 65, 74
Madagascar 10, 11, 14
magic 50
Magpie-lark 79
marimbu 46
Marralam 40
Masters, Dr Bernadette 72
Meda Station 67
Mermaid, HMC 16, 63–5
Mermaid Tree 63–6
Messenger 70
mihrab, Islamic 65
Mornington Station 45
mortuary 60
Mount Anderson Station 60
Mount Barnett 68
Mowanjum 41
Mueller, Ferdinand, Baron von 16–17, 19, 71
Mulvien, Anne Carmel 51
muruwan 37
myth 50–1

names
  indigenous 37
  scientific 16–19
Nangan, Joe 51
Nankeen Kestrel 79–81
Ngaliwuru 37
ngipi 37
Nillibubbica 53
Ninety-east Ridge 14
North Australian Exploring Expedition 17, 42–3, 68–71
Nungali 37

Obern, Ian 67
Olngorru 49
Oscar Range 55
Owenia reticulata 43
Owlet-Nightjar 82

Pandilo, Mary 44–9
Pascoe, Mary Jane 74, 77
Paspaley Pearls 76
Peasley, Dr J. 66
Percy, Patrick 54
Pike, Jimmy 84, 90

pollination 15, 24–7
Principal camp 69
Prison Tree
  Derby 58–60
  Wyndham 60

Queensland 40
Quinlan, E. 76

resin 43–4
Ryder, Darcy 60–1

Scott River 15
Seychelles Islands 15
Sheep Island 73–7
Sholl, R. J. 73–5
Sholl, Treverton 74
Simon, Biddy 40, 48
Species plantarum 16
Spencer, Alison 66
Stokes, John Lort, R. N. 66–7
Swart, E. R. 20

Tawny Frogmouth 83
Timor 69
Toilet Tree 57
Tom Tough 43, 68–9
Tomkinson, T. 76
tools, stone 68, 84
Tragedy Tree 60
transplantation 35
tsingy plateaux 15

uses, indigenous 37–50

Victoria River 54, 68, 72

wajarri 37
wallaby, rock 30
warnda 46
water storage 31, 38
Watson, John 60
Wedge-tailed Eagle 51
Woodman, John 76
White-faced Heron 81
Wickens, G. E. 16
Willing, Tim 19, 29, 43, 65, 66

Zebra Finches 81